"Sharon CassanoLochman's words speak directly to my heart, instigating profound insights into my own struggles and victories. She truly is a Spiritual Warrior who has gained enormous wisdom through every battle won and those lost."

—**Mary B. Love**, *Author*

Spiritual
Verse Today

God's Light

VOLUME I

SHARON CASSANOLOCHMAN

To my son, Christopher Lee Cassano—
never far from my heart.

Dedicated to the memory of Sandra Knope. May the
legacy of her compassion live on through our actions.

Table of Contents

Gratitude to God *Embrace Differences* 1

Words Straining to Flee *Cadence Needed.* 2

Walk with God *Life's Storms.* 3

Alone at Your Desk *Journeyman Days near the End* 4

Heavenly Warrior *Peace Needed* 5

Drama and Chaos *Spiritual Well* 6

Free-Spirited Butterfly *Keeper of Light* 7

One Less Tick Upon the Clock *Passing of a Loved One* 8

Praying for Answers *Magnitude of Cries* 9

Earthly Obligations *Forever be Joyful* 10

Surrender to Your Sorrow *Shadowed Darkness.* 11

Playful Living *Company of Others*. 13

Mission Statement *Live Life by Example* 14

Uniting in Faith *Children of God* 15

We are One *Speaker Teacher Preacher Writer* 16

Gratitude for God's Blessings *Beauty of the Moment* 17

Perfection to Your Core *Breath of God Gave Life*. 18

Haze of Life *Life's Journey* 20

Clouded Mirror *Brilliant Beauty* 21

Shattered Health *New Realizations*. 22

Industrialized Sleep *Balance for Humanity* 23

Emotional Ties *Strength from the Universe* 25

Refuge in God's Blessings *Cowardly Chatter* 26

New Beginnings *Let in the Light* 27

Messages of Hope *Words Unhindered* 28

Minding the Gate *Love Yourself and Neighbors* 29

Journal with the Mind *Blessings of Nature*. 30

Child of God *Let Go of the Past* 31

Gratitude this Holiday Season *Prayerful Wishes*. 33

Moments of Uncertainty *Harmonious Intentions*. 34

Times of Struggle *Pray for Strength*. 35

Stress *Butterfly Light* 36

Ignorance of Youth *Forever of Tomorrows* 37

Sit Watch Click *Child's Play.* 38

Pray for Miracles *Pink Pinafores and Overalls* 39

Blanket of Light *Depths of Depression* 41

Let God Carry Your Burdens *Seek Personal Peace* 43

Heavenly Goal *Seek God* 44

Accept the Journey *Words for the Writer* 45

Darkness *Unite in Light.* 46

Beautiful Soul *Friend.* 47

Knowledge *Honor God.* 48

Wedged on the Threshold *Amazing Life Awaits.* 49

False Surface *Hidden Shame.* 50

Sorrowful and Listless *The Perplexities of Life* 51

Time of Need *Midst of Fire* 52

Fear of Heartache *Allow God's Light.* 53

Search with Your Heart *Compassion* 54

Believe *Good Deeds* 55

Tender Messages *Write Speak Sing Praise* 56

False Smiles *Expense of Another* 57

Wedged to the Past *Pray* 58

Harsh Tone *Trumpets across Nations* 59

Topsy-Turvy *Hold Firm with Grace* 60

Love Freely Given *God by Your Side* 61

Empty Belly *Sustainability* 62

Blaming and Excuses *Forgiveness Love Compassion* 63

Nourish Your Soul *Strive for Spiritual Health* 64

Surge of Words *Release Fear* 65

Door of Possibilities *Amazing Life Awaits* 66

Slippery Depth *Ego's Sanctions* 67

Challenges Unannounced *Walk in God's Light* 68

Sorrow to Shed *Heartbeat of Humanity* 69

Scuffles with Thought *Compassion and Forgiveness* 70

Drudgery of Life *Child's Play* 72

Challenges Faced *God's Light* 73

Restless Sleep *Awake* 74

Sacrifices Made *Sorrowful Cries* 75

Stammering and Sputtering *Issue Repeats* 76

Free as a Spring Butterfly *Released* 77

Once Majestic Nation *Way of Life* 78

Memories Cycled *Forgiveness* 80

Distinctions Unique *Perfection Inside and Out* 81

Pink Leopard Sunrise *Give Gratitude* 83

Trembling of Faith *Pray* 84

Gratitude *Union with God* 85

Gifted of God *All Living Things* 86

Joyful Existence *Pleasures Traveled* 87

Spring Flower *Perfection* 88

Absence of Judgment *God's Love* 89

Weight of Another *Humility and Compassion* 90

Take Your Sorrow to God *Comfort through Prayer* 91

Drifting to Monotony *Moments Unknown* 92

Compassion over Reaction *Rocky Path Taken* 93

Renewed Faith *Glorious Butterfly* 94

Facing Tragedy *Stronger than You Think* 95

Emotional Fields *Peace and Tranquility* 96

Borrower of Words *Blessings Shalom Aho Amen* 97

New Beginnings *Release to God* 99

Shadow Cast *Eternity* 100

Faithful Service *Constant Diligence* 101

God's Creation *Exceptionally Different* 102

Lost Connections *Gifted Conversation* 103

Inhaling Life's Blessing *Unswaggering Intention* 104

Wall of Silence *Conversation Gifted* 106

A Mother's Love *Watercolor Celebrations* 107

Burdens Placed *Dignity of You* 108

Human Connection *Blaming* 109

Loneliness *Fullness of Heart* 111

Sunrise Promise *Good on the Horizon* 112

God's Gift *Life's Drum* 114

Grief Suffering Sadness *Humbly Embrace Life* 115

Contribution to Humanity *Simple Acts of Kindness* 116

Beacon of God's Light *Linking of Hearts* 118

Calming Waters *Life's Challenges* 119

Emotional Cleansing *Release to God* 120

Abundance Gifted *Search with Your Heart* 121

Peaceful Existence *Amazingly Beautiful* 122

Love of the Father *Surrender to Serenity* 123

Life Gifted *Through the Looking Glass* 124

Stuttering of Pen *Gift of God* 125

Sadness of Heart *Past Traveled* 126

God's Love *Beauty and Innocence* 127

Toil Happily *Seriousness with Moderation* 128

Mind Still Strong *Rainbow of Innocence* 129

How to Judge Success *Eliminate Comparisons* 130

Show God to a Child *Faith* 131

Sufferings of the Heart *Wishes and Prayers* 132

Future in Hand *Perpetuate Peace* 133

Follow God's Light *Calm Waters*. 134

Reigning Sovereign *Look beyond Yourself*. 135

Distractions *Enjoy the Moment*. 136

God is not a Politician *Gentle and Sweet*. 137

News Reports and Polls *Lost in Translation*. 138

Promise Given *Knowing and Believing* 139

Overcome Aging *Learn to Love Life* 140

Power of Prayer *Lighting a Path* 141

Media's Distortions *Be Bold*. 142

Precious Moments Lost *Hope for Today* 143

Empty Promises *False Voices*. 144

Lost Second Chance *Faith* 145

Tears Concealed *Journey of Grief* 146

Open Your Heart *Walk in God's Light*. 147

Abandonment *God's Love*. 148

Preacher Speaker Writer Teacher *Gentle Soul*. 149

Life Lessons Learned *Stumbles* 150

Forgiveness Gifted *Seeds of a Dandelion* 151

Focus on God's Light *Shadowed Images* 152

Angst Blankets Our Nation *Prayer and Intention* 153

Dream Sing Dance Write Draw *Mind Heart and Soul*. . . . 154

Dream *Path of Prayer*. 156

Passing of a Loved One *Forever Missed*. 157

Pollyanna Pink Sunset *After the Fight*. 158

Disruption *Spotlight Brilliance*. 159

Joyful Reunion *A Lifetime of Love* 160

Wake-Up Call *Live Life*. 161

Speakers Teachers Writers Preachers *Path to God*. 162

Author's Note

We sit at the helm of opportunity. The opportunity of change. Change from hardened hearts to the awareness of God's love. Change from discrimination to the love for neighbors regardless of color, creed, or location. Change from poverty and starvation to a world nourished with good intentions. Change from abuse to gifted conversation. Change from pollution to a cleaner planet.

Gifted we all are with specialized talents. Use your God-gifted abilities and take the opportunity to change our planet. Grab hold of the helm. Everyone is needed.

—Sharon CassanoLochman

GRATITUDE TO GOD

Embrace Differences

So testy and agitated you are of late. Impatient and belittling of strangers and friends. Attitude towards choices *they make.* How to talk, walk, dress, and eat. So much time wasted questioning and judging the actions and decisions of others. Stop trying to remold them as you. Look to what you deem as a fault, instead as a gift from God. Uniqueness is His specialty. Allow for dignity in differences.

Needed are procrastinating dreamers to see life through visions. Needed are take-charge doers birthing visions to action. Needed are nitpicking detailers delivering action to fruition. Needed are kind-hearted souls bridging the gaps.

Balancing energies is embracing humanity. Each person on this planet has *their* place. Thanks to God—we are all *not* the same. Look to the differences with joy and compassion. Pick up the slack and honor their gift, as well as your own.

Dream—do—think—connect. It will be for the greater good of all.

WORDS STRAINING TO FLEE

Cadence Needed

I witnessed the tragedy. Heartbroken was I. For you stopped midstream. Your heart raced happily with words straining to flee. But fear of those near silenced your song.

My friend, it is not the tune or the tone of life, but the intention of the song. Perfect it need not be. It is the intention of life's hymn that raises vibration for all. Your cadence is sorely needed.

Sing through life. Through times of sorrow and times of joy. Live your life in song. Be free. Join with me. I'll be singing the loudest. Perhaps out of tune—but in harmony.

WALK WITH GOD

Life's Storms

I see the weather of life etched across your face. Eyes once bright, now dim in Light. Courage gone from a heart once brave. My friend, look past this moment. You have life.

With life is gifted the possibility of change. Change of situations. Change of direction. Change of emotions. Change of dynamics within relationships. Simply—change.

Lift your frail hand, if but one finger at first. Reach for life with all that you have. It is your life. It is your breath. Take this opportunity to change the climate of your life.

Walk with God. Allow God to provide direction and safe passage through life's storms.

Child of God, you have been gifted a life to enjoy. A life to Shine. Shine in God's Light. Be all. Do all. Give gratitude for the opportunity to change. In this moment, you have life. Waste not this precious gift.

The past is the past. Look not back to steps taken. Look forward to the possibilities of a peaceful existence.

See, feel, and believe. There is hope, my brave friend. Have courage. Take this first step forward.

ALONE AT YOUR DESK

Journeyman Days near the End

Sheepishly you struggle. Alone at your desk. Placement of tones and phrases assessed. Unable to recognize the value of efforts placed. My friend, we were not born knowing how to write. There is a curve of learning all writers endure. Patience and hard work. It will pay off in the end. I promise. For written words continue to live.

Long past the visit with your pad and pen, continue on will your phrases through the hearts and minds blessed to connect. Face the fears of the process. Technique mastered. Journeyman days are nearing the end.

Embrace your projects with attitude changed. To be a master requires patience, time, and hard work. Enjoy the process. For you pass through this moment only once.

HEAVENLY WARRIOR

Peace Needed

Heavenly warrior, you are indeed. Majestically speaking. Actions driven from your heart-place. Shine brightly, my friend. Go forward with strength. Ignore the bantering from those heavily drugged from ego's sleep. Speak. Write. Engage. Create. Teach by example through words and actions. Human you are. With a crooked-trail past. Model of spiritual growth with good actions seeded.

Shine, for you will guide souls drowsy from sleep. Waking in the dark. Searching for Light. Joining the many. Hand to hand. Heart to heart. Regardless location, religion, or nation. Gaining momentum. Beacons stepping forth from every direction. Beacons of peace. Beacons of Light.

Warrior of Light. Compassionately driven. Shine.

DRAMA AND CHAOS

Spiritual Well

I understand the space in which you sit. Drama and chaos swirling and churning. Uneven footing and off-balance throughout. Moments of magnificence going unnoticed. Exhausted. Drained.

My friend, time to fill your spiritual well. Take a walk. Slow in motion. Matters not the location. God's graces everywhere abound. Breathe deeply. Fill your lungs with fresh air. Even on a blustery day, you will feel God's gentle kiss upon your face. Seek these moments to fill yourself with peace.

When approaching that rocky emotional cliff, heed these words. Look up. Breathe. Reach for the Heavens. Give gratitude for the glorious day. Then dance through life's rocky precipice with ease and grace.

FREE-SPIRITED BUTTERFLY

Keeper of Light

Stunning you are. Carefree. Content. Pre-owned appearance now disappeared. Years of stress no longer visible.

Hardships endured. Freedom rewarded. Independent and self-sufficient. Uncabled at the ankle. Able to fly on your own.

A remarkable transformation into a free-spirited butterfly. Blinding brightness radiating from within. A Keeper of God's Light.

Soaring high.

ONE LESS TICK UPON THE CLOCK

Passing of a Loved One

I am so sorry to learn of your loss. Time will heal.

Traditional clichéd sympathy cards hardly begin to appease the depths of your sorrow. You travel your day keenly aware that life still goes on. Couples laugh, cars stop at traffic lights, people mindlessly shop, carefree individuals litter the streets, playful children run happily, and the birds still chirp.

How dare they be so oblivious to the sadness you carry.

How dare your loss go unnoticed.

My friend, this passing did not go unnoticed. God feels your pain. It is a pain that is shared and carried through the vastness of the Universe. Did you not feel the Earth's hesitation? Did you not know there was one less tick upon the clock?

I *am* sorry to learn of your loss. Time *will* heal.

May you find God through prayer. Peace will then follow.

PRAYING FOR ANSWERS

Magnitude of Cries

Sorrow fills your days. Shocked and dismayed. The phone call most feared. No warning. Seldom is.

Passing the day, robotic in motion. Wishing the planet to stop spinning. Heartbroken. Lost forever are the *love you more*, and horn beeps *good-bye*.

Alone in togetherness. Praying for peace. Praying for time to pass quickly. Praying for answers why. Not yours. Not this sweet thing. Lost in time. Snuffed out in the prime. Forever peaceful. Forever young.

Words will not heal or replace that which was taken. God alone understands the magnitude of your cries. Your wailing moments throughout the darkness of day.

God has left in the empty space a promise of eternity. Life everlasting.

Let the tears flow. When ready, gather the remnants of the day. Look for peace in the beauty of the moment. Sunset sky. Rain. Gentle breezes. Pray for guidance. Pray for peace. Pray for patience. You shall be together again.

EARTHLY OBLIGATIONS

Forever be Joyful

I recognize your challenges. So much to do within the limits of an earthly lifetime. Agility of a hummingbird required.

Take care of your body. The spirit will follow. Nourishment and leisure of the moment are required to maintain the schedule.

Again you pause, disbelief forever creeping in the darkened caverns of fear.

Doubt will sacrifice your journey. Are you willing to stop now? Think not. Just do. The more you learn, the faster the momentum will flow.

Judge not the obstacles on your earthly path. Have you not learned that those bumps are the lessons needed to bring you closest to God?

Look to your earthly obligations with peace. Joyfully live, work, and play.

Stop not. You've been gifted this lifetime.

Waste not. You've been gifted this lifetime.

Forever be joyful. Forever be kind and compassionate. Forever be the best, do the best, love the most, laugh the longest, live your life to the fullest. Forever.

This is your gift. Waste not.

SURRENDER TO YOUR SORROW

Shadowed Darkness

I see the shadowed darkness of your woundedness. Cloaked with insecurities and self-doubt, sequestered from joyful expressions and opportunities.

You gave love freely, but mistakenly to the wrong person. A person more interested in the trinkets of life and immediate gratification. A person consumed with self-indulgent behavior. A person incapable of matching the purity of your love. Are those not *their* deficiencies instead of yours?

Love is more than an emotion. It is the essence of our Being. It is programmed into every cell of our body. We fail to thrive without it.

In a healthy relationship, love is matched equally, wholly, and purely. It is more than the bond between lovers. Love is the ability to intimately share and care for another; to tenderly caress their soul with compassion and gentleness. To *see* them for all that they are and all they can be.

Love is not manipulation or exploitation. Love is not needy or greedy. Love is not regimented to a clock or meant to be crammed into a box of opportunity.

Love is the silhouette of our Creator.

Embrace tightly the knowledge that when you are ready, you command the ability to cut the strings that emotionally bind you to the other.

You are not to blame. Your love was given deeply, intensely, and innocently.

Surrender to your sorrow and move on.

Company of Others

Speak not to me of your latest distress. Pacing and peeking. Wringing of hands. Drawing your shades to increase the distance. Tormenting angst by your own wishes. Seething and spewing. Conversations limited to the *idiots* next door. Complaining *they* play as children.

I'm tired of listening.

How long has it been? How long has it been since you enjoyed the company of others? Playful and innocent exchanges.

Difficult to say the best way to reply. So long it has been—you can't remember when. Turn from watching the activities of others. Start with conversations. Well wishes will follow. Smile at their antics. It is joyful living. Good for the soul. Good for theirs. Good for yours.

Open your blinds or keep them closed. The choice is yours. But please consider playful living of a joyous sort. Happier you'll be as a better neighbor and friend. Life is too short. Life is for living.

I'm heading next door to introduce myself. Coin me an *idiot* or travel in tote.

Live Life by Example

Hidden shame. You are not alone. Learning occurs in spurts of curves. Through our decisions, inner knowing is gifted. A sense of this, not that.

Let go of shame. Hold the lesson learned. When heavy in heart, experiment with solitude. Close to home. Close to God. And when you must go out, mind the inner compass. A sense of this, not that. Let God discern your heavenly path. Allow the gentle guiding to possibilities.

Recognize choices that insult your time and talents.

Challenging days ahead. Yes, it is agreed life will not be easy. But joyful you shall remain if settled within the moment. Trust the path, even when it seems dead-ended.

Be good. Do good. Spread good. Shall that be your life's mission statement. Live life by example.

UNITING IN FAITH

Children of God

Inclusivity is the task. Outreaching parameters of space or creed. Narrowing caverns of race and religion. Uniting in faith of a power greater than ourselves. Uniting in heart and then in hand. Walking single file is not the way, but sharing of paths with intersecting lessons. Holding and carrying hearts united is the better way.

Offensive behavior generates from fear and ignorance. Fear of that which is unknown. Ignorance of similarities between peoples. Take time to acknowledge your neighbor. Next door and across the sea. Agreement with which shoe to tie first no longer an issue with the realization that all have feet.

Preachers, teachers, writers, and speakers. Use your skills gifted. Chant unity of hearts for varieties of differences. For beauty is in all God's creations. Regardless parameters of space or creed.

WE ARE ONE

Speaker Teacher Preacher Writer

I commend your diligence. Sequestered from society—your gifts break cycle. Phrasings from the heart gathering momentum. Releasing caged knowledge.

Your energy rises. Gifted words from above. Quickly written. Time is short. You were late for roll call.

Words setting the foundation for the union of hearts. Significant in this place and time that lacks goodwill and compassion. A reminder is needed that we are one.

Alone you sit penning philosophies. Spreading contagious intentions of benevolence. A virus worth catching. Much depends on the weight you carry.

Catch up you must. Remember—you were late. Then confirm with your actions the verses set to paper.

Beauty of the Moment

Life is short. Why so serious? Busy working at life. Life works you. Take a momentary hiatus. Give gratitude.

Give gratitude for nature. For neighborhoods and communities. For the opportunity to be a friend.

Give gratitude for life in all forms. Beauty abounds. So abundantly grand.

Give gratitude for this day gifted. Simple in form. Unique from all others.

Life is short, my friend. The glory of a moment forever gone with the blink of an eye. Remembrance ensured with gifted gratitude.

PERFECTION TO YOUR CORE

Breath of God Gave Life

Yₒu are a rock.
Rough-surfaced from nature's tribulations. Dotted with darkened hues contrasted by Light. Tossed and turned. Molded by the elements of life.

Like a rock you once were. From the Earth, you came. Breath of God gave life.

No longer resembling that which you once were. The elements have changed you. Rough, cracked, and worn. You could not control your molding any more than the rock.

Waste time no longer looking to the past with sadness or anger. It was. You are. Regardless of the elements. Rise above life challenges. Learn to be. Learn to see. See the perfection carried within a rough surface.

The rock is still the rock in all its manipulations. The core remains the same. *Smash it* you say, as life has smashed you. Shatter it to a million pieces. But each piece still holds perfection to the core. Regardless of size or dimension. Likewise for you. Regardless of how many times your heart has been broken; how many times you've been hurt by another; how many times you've look for, wanted, or needed—your core is still perfection.

HAZE OF LIFE

Life's Journey

You awake, eyes still crusted with sleep as you strain for clarity through the haze of life. You have been gifted nature at its best. Learn to see these gifts. These were donations from Heaven. Gifts from your soul to lighten earthly steps. Learn to listen to the whispers in the wind.

Time to awaken from *reality* and step into your heavenly dream. Be grateful for all souls passed and intersected along the way. Change will come in the form of peace and tranquility.

Peace to you. Safe travels.

CLOUDED MIRROR

Brilliant Beauty

Reach out to hold—wish I could. Time and space dictate. Your suffering apparent. Days spent beating a wall of continuance length. Branches of words that block and twist. Confined in one spot. When will it be enough? Choices and paths can be undone. Of great importance are the talents you wear. The place in which you sit is by your plan. Tolerance on your part to some degree. Seeking reinforcement of pity and low self-esteem. My dear, you are glorious! Can't you see?

Never allow words or actions of another define that which you are and that which you can be. You are a child of God. You are Light. Grace. Purpose. Your talents are desperately needed. Until you see the value of you, the wall stands tall. Perfectly masoned. Reinforced by your feelings of insignificance.

Swipe clean the clouded mirror. See your brilliant beauty begging to shine. A magnitude of possibilities is just beyond.

SHATTERED HEALTH

New Realizations

I miss you. The you I once knew. Sharing laughter and dreams—so innocent. Anger and frustration now rule your existence. Shattered health shatters your life. Depression swallows your days and births fitful nights.

There's good to be found regardless the situation. Find courage. Rage war against hurling impediments. Find peace. Peace for the moment. Limitations unnoticed. Distractions abandoned. Make the best. Be the best. Life is to be shared. Guidance offered for those inexperienced with hardship. Spread uplifting energy in a feasible form.

Shattered dreams and expectations replaced with new realizations. What do you wish to be remembered for? Shattered health or heavenly direction?

INDUSTRIALIZED SLEEP

Balance for Humanity

Dialogue closing. Action to be taken. Time at hand to wake the many. Shaking them from an industrialized sleep. Passing one day to the next. Drawing a paycheck—yet never making ends meet. Wasted energy from one day to the next. When the journey ends, nothing more than blank pages are left.

Meditate.

Put your energy into that which cannot be seen. Balance of self. Connection to a Higher Being. Balance for the whole of humanity awaits.

Meditate.

Release the fear of lacking potential. For within is carried all that is needed. With fear released comes the awareness of peace. Opportunities present. Directions noted. Pleasures taken. Dear one, fear severs and hope heals.

Hope spreads through words compassionately spoken. Hope spreads through actions compassionately gifted. Positive action now taken will reflect for generations yet to come.

Burdensome work. Yes, indeed. Healing and hope for humanity. Time at hand to wake the many.

Strength from the Universe

Stand tall. Outstretch your trembling arms. Draw strength from the Universe. Cut the emotional ties shackled to your ankles. This is your life. Your journey. You are uniquely gifted with many talents. Take care, for there's risk in not being yourself. Risk in giving all and having nothing left.

Unlock the paddock to your destiny. Release yourself to dreams and goals. Leave the mundane. Take that leap. For without the leap you will never fly. Child of God, spread your wings. Amazingly talented you are in so many ways.

How sad it would be at the end of this life if corralled your dreams remained. For each day is a glorious gift. Waste not one moment on falsities and flagrantly artificial goals. You are amazing. The trail you blaze is bold and unique.

Let your Light shine. In your true glory, you live each day with purpose and meaning. Perfect child of God. Reach for the sky. Draw from God's graces.

Let your Light shine.

REFUGE IN GOD'S BLESSINGS

Cowardly Chatter

I know you're heartbroken. Please remember, people that lack character and courage to self-reflect are those that seem to have the most to say.

The clusters of individuals contributing to the cowardly act of gossip are as guilty as the ones initiating the *chatter*. Their guise of bold and arrogant courage is merely a facade as they spinelessly chirp from the cloak of anonymity. If there's no one to listen—the chatter will stop.

Remove yourself from the spotlight. Take refuge in the blessings God has provided. Turn off the volume from idol minds and ignorance. Feel God's love embrace you during your lonely moments.

You know the truth. Stay strong and balanced.

Family and friends that truly care will remain close at heart—and silent.

NEW BEGINNINGS

Let in the Light

Complaints you make. Situation stagnant. Agitated and uncomfortable with the organization of life. Piles scattered about. Stubbing your toes on stacked boxes of sorrow and self-pity. Tripping over files of unrealized best intentions. Panes of your life heavy and clouded.

Life is a cycle of ups and downs. Learn to enjoy the power of the moment. Let go. Clean out the dark moments. Unlock and gently wipe clean the panes of your life. Start small. One inch at a time. Sit quietly. Relinquish the *I'll never do that again*. Sometimes the most painful boxes buried and sealed allow in the most Light when released. Give to God the memories blocking your view. A clearer path ahead when you make room for new experiences. Throw out unneeded and unnecessary leftovers of painful situations. Unclutter your space. Unclutter your mind. Lessons kept. Pain released.

Cleansing occurs when you let go. Look not to the whole but to progress made. One inch at a time. Stubbed toes and tripping—a thing of the past. Bright Light, new beginnings, and best intentions now realized.

Words Unhindered

You are a borrower of words. Words gifted from God for you to share. They are not yours to judge or covet. Do not cling to them as earthly trinkets. You are solely the messenger. This is your Light.

Do not waste time tending what does not belong to you. Write and release them. There is a purpose to all that you do. Patience. Time. Motivation. Your efforts will cultivate the seeds planted.

Send forth heartfelt messages of hope. Allow your words to scatter untethered by time or space. Cast them to the wind to be carried on the wings of angels. They belong to the souls that await the message. Your words have a destiny.

Preacher. Speaker. Teacher. Writer. Allow your words to take flight.

MINDNG THE GATE

Love Yourself and Neighbors

I understand your shame. Sometimes life backfires. Truth be told, you minded the gate of your neighbor instead of your own. You were caught up and called out.

Worry not, dear one. You were not gifted a life script. You are here for life lessons. Reflect—then forgive. Forgive yourself for meddlesome actions. Learn to look within. Mind your front gate—that which comes in and especially that which goes out.

Forgiveness of yourself is the hardest to master. The more you reflect, the easier it becomes. Compassion and understanding for past actions done. Move forward. Love yourself and your neighbors.

JOURNAL WITH THE MIND
Blessings of Nature

Important it is. Acquainting children with God through more than mere verse. Go to the source. Expose God in the harmony of backyard nature. Walk lightly upon the earth. For in your footsteps they will follow. Observation without direction. Peaceful reflection of God's blessings. Teach to seek and listen. Quiet observers of harmony in nature.

Journal with the mind. Translate to the heart. Everything holds beauty and purpose. Everything holds perfection. Touched by God. Given breath.

Acquaint yourself with God. Regardless of age. Words are not enough. Needed is God's hand upon your heart. Add to your verses God's harmony and blessings of nature.

CHILD OF GOD

Let Go of the Past

Helplessly I watch as you waste a lifetime seeking that which will never come.

Approval.

Confirmation.

Love from those now departed.

You seek that which was never realized. Adulthood spent tending the leftovers of your youth. You tend *their* possessions better than your parents tended you.

Matters not how the details of your life are manipulated and misconstrued, past or present. You are a child of God. Your parents were merely guardians. Job done well or not; it takes not away from *you*. A child of God. Beautiful and cherished you have always been.

Hold not onto that which will never come. The disappointments of your upbringing will not be sufficed through things—but through actions.

Let go of the past. Tend the child within. Seek peace in your heart. Dance carefree to the songs of the wind. Release the urge to hold onto. Release kindness to others. Release kindness to yourself.

You are a child of God. Beautiful and cherished as you have always been.

GRATITUDE THIS HOLIDAY SEASON

Prayerful Wishes

Change of focus required. Holiday void family or friends. Untended lapse of time. Darkness cowers in the corner. Sadness dominates. Unpacked glassware of heart's memories. Boxed. Sealed.

Change of focus greatly needed. Swallowed and consumed with that which is missing. But what of that which is?

Look about. Surely there's more *ofs* than *missings*.

Grace silk ribbon with words or phrases. Gratitude given. Prayerful wishes. Attach to pine branches. Tended moments spent in gratitude gently exchanged.

Look about. What is it that brings you peace? Clean water? A bed to sleep? Grace your silk ribbons. Give gratitude for this day gifted.

MOMENTS OF UNCERTAINTY

Harmonious Intentions

Dab those misused tears away. Tears are for joy and happiness. Not squandered moments and paths mistaken.

Life choices forever vary. Options changing like angelically strummed wind chimes. Never the same.

Straddle these precious moments of uncertainty. For during the unsettledness comes clarity. Play a new song within the breath of life. Conductor you are. Orchestrating mesmerizing tones. Delicately whispered to listening souls. Gifted to humanity.

Strum your song, my friend. Send each exhale back to the Universe with harmonious intentions. Tears welcomed with heartfelt connections made. The magnificence of life, overwhelming at times. So much joy, peace, and tranquility to be had in each moment.

TIMES OF STRUGGLE

Pray for Strength

I search with my heart and feel your pain. Everything in order. Then chaos reigns. Disheveled and torn. Brought haphazardly to your knees. Life happens. Through times of struggle—step back. Step back from the chaos. Pray for strength.

Renew faith in yourself. Renew faith in God. Recognize God's blessings tightly wrapped.

Guarantees were not given that life would be easy. It is the ability to remain balanced in God's love that makes the difference. Renew your faith in times of struggle. Carry your faith through the remainder of your days.

STRESS

Butterfly Light

Stress varies in shape and form. Dark storm clouds billow and bluster in and about. Passing eventually. Don't feed it, for stress wraps and steals butterfly light.

Butterfly light directing new beginnings. Fresh starts. Intuitive ideas. Pleasant thoughts. Butterfly light delicately fluttering. Lacing together hopes and dreams. Dusted with possibilities. Twinkling with heavenly Light.

Stress is better left to itself. Ignored and relinquished to the back door. Let go of that which has overtaken your life. Look to God's graces and the butterfly light.

IGNORANCE OF YOUTH

Forever of Tomorrows

So common it is. Pointing the finger. Observant and quick to morally sentence. Acknowledgement of what is missed or discerned from others. Ignorance of youth. Arrogantly living with a forever of tomorrows.

My friend, what about you? What splendid experiences have you missed just today? It is not solely the ignorance of youth. It is ignorance of you. What certificate of guarantee is there for any tomorrows?

Would not the better way be to stop looking out and look *in*? If this is the last, then with all your heart from gratitude speak. Thank you for sunrises and sunsets. Thank you for every substance of love and learning this life has afforded. With focus on gratitude—in front—within—and behind—how differently things seem.

The importance of the moment when the moment is all there may be.

My friend, live your life with gratitude and grace. Recognize each and every significant moment.

SIT WATCH CLICK

Child's Play

When was the last time you let your children play? Not with video games or computerized communications. When was the last time you witnessed true child's play? Dirty hands and feet caked in mud. Sloppily washing pretend dishes. Building a city of sandcastles. Jumping rope. Absence of thirty-minute increments.

When was the last time you let yourself play?

I see where your children learned to sit, watch, and click. Watch a screen varying in size and function. Click on the keyboard, cellphone, remote, or controller.

Shame on you for letting your children go without. Without fresh air filling their lungs. Without dancing, jumping, and laughing outdoors. Without the pleasure of Earth Mother under their feet.

Dear friend, how can you teach what you've forgotten? Reacquaint yourself with child's play. Then take your children to the great outdoors. Teach them deep breaths. Teach them to take off their shoes and run along a sandy beach. Teach them respect. Respect for clean air and a place to play. Respect for the absence of time.

PRAY FOR MIRACLES

Pink Pinafores and Overalls

Welcomed you were to this earthly place. Your soul full of hope for the journey at hand. Lessons to learn. Full of God's grace. Earliest innocence of pink pinafores, overalls, and footie pajamas. Consumed now with adult remedies of the most treacherous kind. Forcing sleep onto a most innocent. Friends dreaming of first loves, prom dates, and colleges. Whilst you strive for the next fix.

Deserving you are of the abundance of all sorts. Happiness, peace, and love. Beautiful you are from the core to exterior. It is not too late. Life begets hope. Hope of a tomorrow free of strife.

Face the devilish hand dealt. Come to terms. Acknowledge. Then sit with yourself. You weren't responsible for the painful infliction. Deserving you were and still are of so much more. Challenges ahead you must face. But stronger you'll be than ever before. With God at your side and free of vice.

You can do this. Everything needed is buried inside. Even

through the darkest of days, a Keeper of God's Light you remain. Pray for passage through the rough spots. Pray for physical relief. Pray for miracles.

I'll pray for the child within. Still wearing pink pinafores, overalls, and footie pajamas. Deserving of first love, prom dates, and college expectations.

The Heavens rejoiced with your first breath inhaled. You are deserving. A wonderful life awaits. You can do this, dear one. Stand strong. Pray.

BLANKET OF LIGHT

Depths of Depression

Depression is the equalizer. Souls taken hostage regardless of social or ethnic status. Slithering forth hidden under the cloak of fear.

Fear of the unknown. Fear of the unfamiliar. Fear of solitude. Fear of loss.

You danced with fear—then depression. Drapes drawn, lights out, alone in the darkness. Feeding fear. Feeding depression.

The Universe embraced you offering comfort within Earth Mother's rocking motion. Morning to night, morning to night, morning to night.

Still blinded, you cried, "Why have all forsaken me?" Friends loved deeply, turned and disappeared. Shadows left of mere memories haunting your daily existence. *Why?* Did you not love enough?

You begged to return to the arms of your Creator. And then. . . .

The faintest Light began to emerge. Your Light. With your head planted upon the bosom of Earth Mother, you grounded yourself within Her strength. You awoke to the enfolding of your soul. Your inner strength emerged.

A miracle was bestowed upon you. A blanket of heavenly light lifted the darkness; leaving in its place God's Light. Peace replaced sorrow. Knowing replaced ignorance. Love and forgiveness filled the empty caverns of your heart.

You are one with God's Light.

LET GOD CARRY YOUR BURDENS

Seek Personal Peace

Saddened I am to see you of late. Huddled spirit. Vision lost. Shortened height. Left to wallowing in an emotional cycle. Caught up. Caught in. Unable to see the Light.

Well-wishes are not enough. Tied are my hands. For resolution, you must look within. The transformation must come from you. Opt for happiness. Seek peace. Seek Light.

I understand the heartache, sorrow, disappointment, and fear. Intimate and personal challenges. Knee-buckling suffering.

Look beyond the darkness for the glimmer of Light. Open your eyes to God's love and affection. Gift to Him the wearisome burden. Wrap your heart about His love. Allow His strength to carry you. Stop struggling on your own. Let God tote the load.

Look not to be forever sad. Seek intimate and personal peace. Happiness and joy will soon follow. Gift your burdens to God.

HEAVENLY GOAL

Seek God

Transgression against you that is true. Hurtful words flagrantly spoken. Anger and hurt transparent across your china-glass face. Recipient of the angry and selfish onslaught of another.

Look to the perpetration with compassion. Step up. Reach high. Hold not to resentful feelings that cycle. Continuance unending. Hurtful to the soul.

Guardian of their ways you are not. They have their path of lessons yet to learn. Peace and compassion within you are essential.

Resentment has a snowball effect. Consuming joy and happiness. Stealing good intentions. Let not the actions of one interfere with the goodness of all. Let not the actions of one take away a smile that could be passed along. Let not the actions of one detract you from your heavenly goal. Sharing, lifting, loving, and giving. You are bigger than that! Your joyful exchange lightens the burdens of souls intersected.

When resentment takes over and compassion wanes—seek God for support.

ACCEPT THE JOURNEY

Words for the Writer

Time passes quickly. I understand and appreciate the fears you face. Self-inflicted doubt and self-sabotage can turn hours into decades. You are a writer. You were gifted this destiny.

Trust yourself. Trust God. Trust in the great and wonderful gift bestowed upon you. Trust and set the words free. Trust and let go. It is your journey.

Have you not gone to works past to revisit old cherished characters and stories? Do not the words continue to bring tears, laughter, or suspense—even though they were birthed from your pen and imagination? Do you not see or feel the magnificence and power of language? Let the words go. Set your stories free.

Trust in your journey.

Please, dear friend. Write . . . write . . . and write some more.

DARKNESS

Unite in Light

Patience required through turmoil and strife. Remember you must. Darkness cowers from Light. Stronger you must hold to truth. Sing louder. Love wider. Clap stronger. Dance longer. Stand taller. For in God's Light you shine. Beyond the dark-hearted individuals will rise an army of heavenly souls. Joined together through prayer. Regardless of location—religion—or nation.

Join in. Sing from your heart-place heavenly hymns. Overcome strife with God's grace. Radiate from within all that is good and decent. We are of one breath. We are of Light. Gloriously radiant. Children of God. Take your place. We shall overcome. Together. United as one. United in prayer. United in song. United in heart. United in Light.

Turn up the volume. Sing from your soul. Dance from your heart. Together. Unite we must in compassion and goodness.

BEAUTIFUL SOUL

Friend

Beautiful soul. The lessons you gift to others are grander than an intersected moment. Grace and appreciation. Forward momentum when facing matters of the heart. Limiting from your vocabulary the words of strife and self-pity.

Beautiful, beautiful soul. Such goodness you possess. Thank you for honoring God. Thank you for honoring yourself. Message for all. Time on this walk is short. Make the most. Make the best. Be the most. Be the best. Shine brightly. For graceful is the walk in God's Light.

Honored I am to call you friend.

KNOWLEDGE

Honor God

Much to be said for the elevation of the mind. Fascination with the complexities of numerical equations and alphabetical relations. You are swimming through a sea thick with knowledge. A lot in your head. Off balance you are, for forgotten is your heart. It is in your heart-place that true knowledge is held. Knowledge of compassion and love from the beginning of time. Understanding of connections from man to nature. Basic, perhaps, but intricately Divine.

Combine the gifts of a mind sharp and focused with a heart soft and compassionate. Fascinations researched and refined for the greater good of the whole.

My friend, scholarly degrees are not enough. How you put them to use is the key to universal power. Balanced you must remain. Within your head and heart. Every dot and dash is here for a reason. Close your books and search for your path with your heart.

WEDGED ON THE THRESHOLD

Amazing Life Awaits

Caught you are. Wedged on the threshold of what was and what could be. Trepidation consuming. Hindering one step from the next. An amazing life awaits. Just around the bend.

Ground to Earth Mother. Feel her rocking momentum. Her gravity's embrace. Feel her energy. From God she was created. Guardian and home. Draw from her grace. Release to the Heavens earthly anchors. Matters not your age or station. One foot forward. The other will follow. You hold in your heart the power to heal.

Gifted from God are second chances. Take a walk on paths unknown. Enjoy the journey. Each step. Each breath. Each moment.

FALSE SURFACE

Hidden Shame

I appreciate the transparency of your mission. Once there I too went. Hiding behind a false surface. My friend, God knows of your decisions past and fitful nights current. Awake. You have always been compassionately embraced.

Unclothe hidden shame. Stand before God in all your nakedness. Allow the Light of God to embrace.

Child of God, so beautiful are you in His eyes. You are here for a reason. Wanted and loved. Regardless of history or self-limiting illusions. Child of God, lift your head to a Universe of possibilities. The power you possess is unlimited.

Share heart and compassion. First with yourself. Then with another. Awake to the blinding Light your carry inside.

Gift to others the real you.

SORROWFUL AND LISTLESS

The Perplexities of Life

I've noticed your state of being. Uncomfortable, sorrowful, and listless. Affixed to a colorless concrete wall. Nothingness in all directions. Existence unnecessarily hard. What robbed you of innocence and life goals?

Reach for the stars instead of a blank wall.

Get your momentum going. Learn to try.

Overcome your sorrow-inflicted limitations. Become a teacher, a friend, a learner. Become a leader.

I'll hold your hand. I'll provide refuge in my heart. Then when you're ready—first steps, dear one, will be on your own. Courage and joy will abound.

Move away from the nothingness and into God's Light.

TIME OF NEED

Midst of Fire

I commend your efforts. Proud I am to call you friend. Courage exemplified in the midst of fire. Determination and sense of something other than self. Quick thinking. Saving lives.

Generous we all must be. Pitching in. Helping out. Disasters happen. Personal and natural. Part of life.

Extending oneself. No questions asked is how we survive.

Thank you for helping another in a time of need.

FEAR OF HEARTACHE

Allow God's Light

Shrouded you inch through life. Wisdom and compassion selfishly concealed. A heart, most tender, sequestered and locked from sight. Draped within layers of mistrust. Craving slumber's sweet embrace.

What a shame. For the emotional sleep you seek denies humanity. Denies a stranger an uplifting emotional exchange. Denies your neighbors, friends, and family of laughter and good times. Denies you the journey of gifted moments. A heart imprisoned is denied God's Light.

Unshroud your heart. Shine with God's Light. Give to others. Good deeds. Compassion. Quality of life. Extend yourself. Shroud fears and mistrust. For a heart consumed with God's Light radiates love.

SEARCH WITH YOUR HEART

Compassion

You passed a homeless person today.

Are you unsettled with the vision of the suffering of another soul or your lack of compassion? *Get a job,* you thought. *The burger shop is hiring.*

Tell me, have you gone without food? Have you gone without shelter? Have you gone without?

Before you answer, let me explain.

There are angels on Earth that walk among us. Not adorned with golden crowns or halos. They are in disguise. They are the humble, peaceful souls.

What if in passing a homeless person today you looked with your heart, instead of your head. Would you feel their pain, their suffering? If you felt with your heart, instead of your head, would you feel their love? Feel their Light?

We are all one. We are all Light. Search with your heart— leave the ego behind.

BELIEVE

Good Deeds

Heart-wrenching state of affairs in our world today. It is not what is known that makes the difference. It is what has been forgotten.

Believe. Believe good deeds shall rise and so shall man. Believe in our ability to do what we should. Take paths straight instead of crooked.

Believe. Believe we'll rise and shine to the occasion. Overcome self-deprecating behavior. Use abilities and gifts to benefit humanity.

Believe. Believe in the kindness residing in each heart to be genuine. Giving up on the whole of humanity is not an option. Free choice yes, we certainly have. Would it not be better if we believed in ourselves?

Believe. Believe in the potential of the human race. Belief starts with one, but is contagious to the whole.

Believe. Believe in peaceful awakenings. Believe in the human race.

Believe, my friend. Believe.

TENDER MESSAGES

Write Speak Sing Praise

I agree. Saint you are not. I understand the concern you have for personal mistakes. Crooked paths taken. Once small in Light.

My friend, holding back is not the way. Stockpiling thoughts and phrases for a better day. Heavenly words left unclaimed. Through your suffering is the connection. The world is full of troubled souls seeking commonality *not* found in a saint. It is hope they seek through gray skies.

Recognize your humanness. Send off your tender messages. Speak with compassion. Sing divine. The essence is not what was . . . but what is. For in within humanness . . . are we not the same?

Share your Light, my friend. Simply write, speak, sing, praise.

FALSE SMILES

Expense of Another

I see the Light. Sloppily concealed. Masquerading as a showman of sorts with your cutting remarks. Always at the expense of another. Behind your back, christened a jerk. False smiles and comradery. Why are you the only one seeing the humor?

If unable to think of others then at least consider yourself. You are a child of God. Tenderly placed upon Earth. Gifted with talents and grace. Held before the rising sun. Hope for humanity. Hope for yourself.

Shed the roles you've played in life. Discard the costumes blocking your Light. Be yourself. Tender and sweet. Attention you will still receive. Contagious behavior of the generous sort.

Look for the *good* in others and find yourself.

When all is said and done, what is it you wish in capital letters across your forehead?

WEDGED TO THE PAST

Pray

Sorry for your narrow vision. You are caught on a wedge. Anchored by the weight of your past. Dear one, when caught in the cycle of *you*, simply look about. See and feel the wonders and glories that abound. If still stuck, look to those that go without. Difficult to be wedged to the past when aware of the need of the many in the now.

Pray for bellies of children to be filled. Pray for abuse in all forms to end. Pray for unity of nations and religions. Pray to console the suffering. Pray for your shackled self to be set free. Open your arms. Open your heart. Feel God's presence. Welcome God into your heart.

Pull free of that which holds you back. Your gifts are needed. Help yourself. Help another. Learn your lessons from the past, and don't look back.

HARSH TONE

Trumpets across Nations

A harsh tone trumpets across nations. People lost within the bold print on paper. Toting verses and amendments. Assumptions made. Human connections faded. Fisted hands pound barren earth. Foul attitudes pollute waters. Everything contaminated.

My friend, a lesson shouted is lost between the spaces. A lesson by example lives forever.

In this time of clouded vision, follow to your heart for the path to be taken. One person can make a difference. Take to the curb your recyclable container. Leave to the propagators their rubbish. Leave to the media and politicians their cyclical momentum. Step to the side. Be your own person. Keep Earth Mother clean. Trumpet love and compassion across nations. Make the human connection. We share the same Father.

Better to be followed for your example than to follow the imagined.

TOPSY-TURVY

Hold Firm with Grace

Cycle we do from one thing to the next. This cause. That race. Life spinning in topsy-turvy waves. Time spent in reflection and close self-examination of our intentions would be better placed. Ground to Earth Mother. Hold firm with grace.

There will always be that which is important. Neglect not the purest of time spent in reflection. Momentary meditations or prayers filtered in throughout the day. Calming and centering. Focusing on the importance of life and the grand scheme of things. Little will matter the irritating tailgater, slow talker, or slanted ego.

For with *prayerful meditation* comes the vision of compassion for differences. Proper placement of importance quiets the reigning ego.

LOVE FREELY GIVEN

God by Your Side

I understand your situation. Love freely given. Others taking hold of that so tenderly gifted. Trampling and spewing. Then recycling to another. Leaving you sick and broken. Your heart and soul left hanging on the laundry line of life. Wrung out. Flapping this way and that. Searching for affection. A hand to hold. Conversation shared. Searching—searching—searching.

When all along, you were never alone. For God walked strongly by your side. Holding your hand. Breaking your falls. Offering solace for your mourning soul.

My friend, gift to God your most tender possessions. Your heart and soul.

Search no longer. Simply look within to never be without love.

EMPTY BELLY

Sustainability

G ifted you are. Vision maintained through child-like eyes. Sustainability. Balance of the natural compassionate incli-nation against greed. Straining of voice from repetitive song. If two apples fill an empty belly, give three. Callused and worn from backs turned. Listening gone. My friend, tired you are. But—you must continue on.

It is the humblest of actions to share. Share abundance beyond pennies and dollars. Share compassion, words of encouragement, and prayers for relief for all concerned. Other peoples. Other nations. Earth Mother. Share your heart—God's greatest blessing.

Sing loudly for all to hear. Regardless their stance with backs turned and listening gone. Sing loudly for the greater good of all.

BLAMING AND EXCUSES

Forgiveness Love Compassion

If blaming and excuses are that which you wish to hold—at the end of your journey you will be empty-handed. Blaming and excuses are substance free. Forgiveness, love, and compassion take form. Passing in grand energy from one soul to another. Crossing time and distance.

Hurtful experiences you will always have. It is the action that follows that is important. What emotions do you wish to wear? Anger and frustration or peaceful existence. Negative thoughts and actions or a heart filled with compassion. Tolerance and forgiveness. Patience and goodness. Preference is yours.

Our Earth walk ends in a blink of an eye. Carry to Heaven a heart fully engaged.

NOURISH YOUR SOUL

Strive for Spiritual Health

Rundown you are. Emotionally drained. The body craves what the heart can't take.

Proper nourishment required for a soul deprived of internal bliss. Take a walk. Smell a flower. Smile to a stranger. Gift something to someone else. Negate returned expectations. Touch a tree. Enjoy nature. Watch children at play.

Resistance relents. Spirit soars. Joyful awakening. The Heavens rejoice. Spiritual health. Take needed time for yourself. Nourish your soul.

SURGE OF WORDS

Release Fear

Unsettled you are of late. Inventing chores. The real work left undone.

What is it that holds you back? Fear the words will not flow? Words sucked through the vastness of nothingness into the empty hole of lazy days and lack of motivation. Fear the messages will not be clear? Abstract meanings flying overhead on the wings of birds. Fear time will run out? Words unsaid and the mission left undone. Fear for corralled ability hankering to be released? Talents carefully concealed and protected from rejection.

My friend, fear is the destabilizer. Unearthing fraudulent truths. Keeping life's blessings at bay. Gifted you are with verse and phrases. The words will never run out. Let go of that which holds you back. Let go of fear. Reap the blessings God has gifted. Ride the surge of words.

DOOR OF POSSIBILITIES

Amazing Life Awaits

I see your hesitation at the door of possibilities. Unsettled in unfamiliar emotional surroundings. Unaccustomed to making decisions as an individual. Uncertain of your abilities. Limiting ideas of unworthiness lay in wait for your first stumble.

My friend, life stumbles can be a good thing. They are the lessons that teach you how to walk on your own and at your own pace. Walk the distance. Then climb ladders. Travel through the door of possibilities despite the stomach rumbles.

Shake up and wake up. You are more powerful than you think. You are in control of your destiny. Use your imagination. Think of all the wonderful possibilities life has to offer. If you will just step into your life and not that of another.

Believe in yourself. Believe in your talents. Believe in God's blessings that follow you through the door of possibilities.

Be free. Let your stomach rumble. Leave the limiting ideas of unworthiness behind. An amazing life is on the other side.

SLIPPERY DEPTH

Ego's Sanctions

Run to where your anger resides. To the slippery depth of you. For the anger you wear is your own and not the doings or sayings of another. Sit and reflect. Ignore the internal dialogue of this and that. For agitation arises at your expense. Overflowing frustration for lack control. It is not your place to dictate language and action, with the exception of your own.

What is missing from view is mirrored right back. Stop looking, arguing, and pushing the limits of dispute. The greatest battle is with you.

My wish would be not that of conformity but comfortability. Comfortability with where you are in the moment of now. Without comparison or judgment. In all your nakedness. Unwrapped from ego and imposed sanctions. For when truly happy with yourself will you set free the egotistical disputes.

Child of God, so beautiful in all your missing and broken pieces. Lift yourself from the dark and hazy existence. Love the person God created. Live to be the person God created. Learn to be without judgment of yourself and others. Learn to self-reflect. How is it you wish to be remembered? Angry or at peace.

CHALLENGES UNANNOUNCED

Walk in God's Light

My heart goes with you. Struggles you wear. Rolled and pleated upon your sleeve. Earthly explanation there is not. Trouble gathers and follows for reasons unknown. You've been through worse. Probably more to come.

Remember, dear one, strength, love, and determination. Greatest assets you have. My hero you've been. Faced with obstacles. Yet you dig in. Try you must this time again. Let not depression or bad luck win. Set your standards high. Fight with all you've got. Fight for happiness, success, and relief from plight. Fight for Light.

Reach deep into the heart-place. Find God. Feel guidance. The daily strumming of what-if holds you back. You can rise above the sadness. You can rise above the emptiness of heart. You can walk in God's Light. Fight for life.

Sit quietly within yourself. Release to God pain and strife. Trust God to bring relief. Trust yourself and the powers you hold. Child of God. Beautiful. Magnificent. Grand. Your talents are desperately needed.

Fight—fight—fight. Push through the darkness. Find God's Light. Peace will soon follow.

SORROW TO SHED

Heartbeat of Humanity

Terrible ordeal. Much sorrow to shed. Go to the water. Feel God's breath. Cling to the heartbeat of humanity through the pounding of waves. Gift to God your burdensome cargo. Tears cast into a woven lavender basket. Released. Fill the empty heart-place with God's embrace.

Time will not heal the broken heart from the loss of a loved one. But time will pass. Busy yourself. You are needed and loved. You are here for a reason. Gifted to many. Loved by all.

Search with your heart. Cling to the heartbeat of humanity. Prayers from the many. Surging through rough waters. Leaving a calming effect.

You need not travel alone within your earthly shell. Take good intentions. Well wishes. Prayerful gifts from many. Take God.

SCUFFLES WITH THOUGHT

Compassion and Forgiveness

You wage a battle internal. Scuffles with thought. Wrapped in a blanket of confining ideals. Justifying the ego's interpretation of the right and the wrong. Whilst absent are the precious dream weaves throughout the midnight hours. This war is unnecessary. This war is with you. Agitation of internal strife. Struggle with self-esteem. Struggle with the wounded you. Struggle with the serpent of assumptions. Struggle with the blindness of blessings.

Let go of verbal weapons. Let go of the ammunition of what was said or done. Aim the direction of your angst internal. Sit with yourself. To what part of the situation is there a lesson? Find compassion and forgiveness for yourself and others. For the battle you fight will take its toll. Stealing happiness. Peace. Contentment.

You are a child of God. Find the glory of you. Stop your

struggle. You are worthy of God's abundance and love. You are worthy of happiness. Let go of the ego. Allow God's love into your heart. You are here for a reason.

Cease with the battles internal. Replace scuffles with peace.

DRUDGERY OF LIFE

Child's Play

Child's play. Important connections. Linking heart to mind. Imagination to creativity. Dreams to reality. Foundation of tomorrows. My friend, child's play is a role for any age.

Think of the activities that brought the greatest pleasure. Reading, sewing, drawing, singing, dancing, pretending, playing. Allow the child within to play games. Revisit hobbies once adored. Release latent talents. Turn dreams into reality.

Set the foundation of tomorrow by living today. Pack time in a sack. Gather the toys. Run to a field, a beach, a bench, a place private or public. Join with friends or sit alone. Remove yourself from the drudgery of life. Permit yourself to play. Play at life. Healing begins when you gift yourself the time. Time to play.

Child's play—for any age.

CHALLENGES FACED

God's Light

My heart aches for the challenges you face. Demeanor in constant change. Distant in thought. Overflowing emotion. Huddled about your knees. Guardian of panicked breaths. Swift deterioration. Facing the darkening skies of stormy weather. My friend, you must ride it out.

A reminder offered. Challenges reign in a life unguarded. Pray for protection from the clouded. Pray for a safe voyage. Look to God's Light.

Always there will be lessons and rough spots. Release to God the burdens carried. Release to God the clouded moments. Release to God, then take back the life gifted. Gifted in talents. Gifted in compassion and love extended.

You are here for a reason. Look to God's Light. Seeker of answers.

RESTLESS SLEEP

Awake

S erenity.
   Patiently I wait. For restlessly you sleep. Tossing and
turning. On the brink.

Patiently I pray. Pray for God's blessings and graces. Pray for
you to find your way.

Awake, my friend. Join hands and hearts with others herd-
ing towards God's Light. When brought to your knees, utopia
reached in God's embrace.

Welcome to the joining of hearts. Welcome to peace and
serenity. Welcome to faith and hope. Welcome to forgiveness
and compassion. Welcome home.

My friend, follow the beacon leading to peace.

SACRIFICES MADE
Sorrowful Cries

My thoughts are with you during this turbulent time. Motives of others manifesting into the burdensome twists and turns of life. Dragging within an aching heart.

Struggle you did to bring them life. Sacrifices made through internal strife. Now they sit in the enemy camp. Faltering expectations. Lost affections. Drawn close to another with misguided intentions. Backs turned, hearts closed, ears deaf to reasoning and your sorrowful cries.

Aching heart is not all that is left. There is another direction. Peaceful visualization of happier times. Their holding of your heart through an innocent smile. Release sorrow. Claim hope. Hope of a happier tomorrow. United again. Warm embraces.

Struggle you did to bring them life. Sacrifices made through internal strife. Release to God that which you cannot undo. Pray for softening of hearts and memories unfolded. Release to God. Release pain and doubt. You did the best that you knew.

Suffer no longer. Find peace within even when locked out.

STAMMERING AND SPUTTERING

Issue Repeats

The issue repeats. You sit at an empty page. Loss of words. Scrambled tones. Stammering and sputtering, barely approaching the edge. Harmony clatters. My friend, allow the pen to run freely along the dips and winds of the page. You are the writer, speaker, teacher, preacher. A borrower of words. A borrower of God's song. Your pen will dictate the pace and your heart the path. You need not suffer your craft. You've simply lost the pace.

Stop fighting with yourself. Stop resisting the pull and twangs of stories untold. Characters deserving birth. Believe in the process of carefully placed letters and notes. Twanging and strumming upon the page. Given life when read or heard.

Matters not the gift. Writing, speaking, teaching, preaching—release your gifted talents. If the issue repeats, allow for stammering and sputtering. It happens. Relax. Regain the pace. Release your gift.

FREE AS A SPRING BUTTERFLY

Released

How sad I was to hear of your situation. Abuse comes in many forms. Mental, physical, financial, and social.

You were an addict, waiting for the next *fix* of niceties validating your self-worth.

Look hard in the mirror. What is it that you see? What do you think God sees?

He sees the glorious Light you carry. He sees your beauty and your passion. Your kindness and your gentleness. He sees your generosity—you give all that you have and all that you are. Sometimes those closest to your heart are the least deserving of your gifts, talents, and love.

Remember, dear one, God's Light shines through the darkest of moments.

Forgive yourself. You didn't do anything wrong. You simply loved and were not loved back.

Set yourself free. Free as a spring butterfly.

ONCE MAJESTIC NATION
Way of Life

A blanket of angst continues to cloud a once majestic nation. Situations arise on the right. Situations arise on the left. Brother against brother. Propaganda unravels the foundation. Diplomacy no longer integrated with the American way of life.

We have a legacy to convey, compassion in our tone of life. Music that prevails from around the world no longer rings harmoniously.

Situations arise on the right. Situations arise on the left. Brother need not be against brother. Complain or change. Which is your direction?

Change not the thinking of others with brash tones, thrown stones, or memorized statements. Change the approach you take on this planet. This is not the time to neglect the personal role taken!

Stand on your own if necessary. Recycle your garbage. Clean up the water. Clean litter strewn highways. Support local farmers. Donate to causes that lift the spirits and nation. Think for yourself. Avoid propaganda. Do the best. Be the best. Honor God and the planet. This is your opportunity to make this nation once again majestic in all directions.

Brother with brother. Nations with nations. Linked together through a common cause to end suffering and starvation. End pollution. Clean up your yard first before shaking a fist at another.

It can be done! My sisters and brothers, do not allow for division. Turn your attention away from the emotional rampage. Lift the blanket of angst that clouds our nation. Remember that we are united through breath. Through God—regardless of color or religion.

Do not wait for someone else to take the reins. The time is now to take responsibility for a healthier planet. The time is now to look to your brother with compassion. It is the American way of life! United we can stand in this glorious nation.

End the drama with action.

MEMORIES CYCLED

Forgiveness

So unnecessary. Squeezing anger from memories that cycle. Rewinding. Replaying. Justification with *but* and *therefore*. Energy and time wasted. Rallying the tender ears of those willing to listen. Swapping and exchanging. A twist here. A thumb to the chin there. What of forgiveness?

Forgiveness is always the easier road followed.

Would not energy be better spent on good deeds and peaceful interactions? My friend, peace follows forgiveness. Cycle then ended.

DISTINCTIONS UNIQUE

Perfection Inside and Out

Understanding I have of this place in which you sit. I was there once. Unsettled with personal distinctions unique. Pointy chin. Ears flapping to the wind. Hair swirling in every direction. Voice whiny and nasally in sound. Drawn away from the reflection in the mirror. Forever wishing for the distinctions of someone else. . . .

. . . until gifted the understanding of true beauty. Swaddling my newborn with pure delight. For my child was born the most beautiful inside and out. What glorious distinctions worn upon a perfect little face. I sat with myself. I looked at my child in disbelief. Innocent beauty tugging at my heart. This perfectly formed Being need not ever be changed. Not even with the chin of mine manifested on this perfectly beautiful newborn's face.

That is when the understanding came. Child of God am I. This is the way God looks at me.

Child of God, beautiful in every way. Carry within your heart the knowledge of your perfection inside and out. Wish not to change one distinction unique. For the glory and beauty of God is manifested in you.

PINK LEOPARD SUNRISE

Give Gratitude

Sarcastically speaking you are of late. Fed up. Stretched out. Angry at God for gifting you life. My friend, too much time wasted wallowing in your own debris. The garbage scattered about is of your own demise.

Blessed are you to wake this day. Blessed with the movement of feet. Step over the anger. Leave behind bad memories. Breathe in new life. Breathe in God's Light.

Face forward. Feet planted firmly on Earth Mother. Witness God's blessings. Uneasy feelings will pass with time. Carry your heart and intentions outside. Wake early. Give gratitude for a pink leopard sunrise. Give gratitude for self-reflection. Give gratitude for change.

Wake up. See the Light!

Pray

Why do you torture yourself? Wringing of hands. Trembling of faith. Fears blinding what the heart already knows. Just pray.

Pray for yourself. Pray for others. You need not know the face, age, religion, or nation. Just pray. Pray for understanding. Pray for a unity of hearts. Pray for peace.

Pray for faith unwavering. Starts with one. Contagious to the many. With prayer is the reminder of our link to God. Our link to Earth Mother. Our link to each other.

Prayer wrapped and swaddled throughout a busy day. Easing temptations. Tender reminders how short our stay. Evoking behaviors of the highest intention. Living a life with grace.

Prayer is communication.

Just pray. Then listen.

GRATITUDE

Union with God

Gratitude. A word easily forgotten. Moments wasted rushing to wrap thoughts and intentions on acquisitions. Loading empty spaces with useless accumulations. Forgetting the powerful word. Gratitude.

Gratitude is the union with God. For with gratitude comes a soft heart. Humble awareness of our place on this planet. A speck of flesh, gifted breath.

Gratitude is the union with God. For we truly cannot be grateful unless we are awake. Awake to see the privilege we have to be alive. Don't waste it. Be grateful.

Gratitude is the union with God. Understanding the power of the four elements that sustain life. We did not just happen upon this place. Give gratitude for the air that we breathe and the water we drink.

Please, never forget, be grateful for life even when the days seem shadowed from Light. Look for God's blessings. From a baby's first smile to the star-dimpled sky.

Gratitude. A powerful word. The more we give gratitude, the more we realize the gift of life.

GIFTED OF GOD

All Living Things

Countless conversations we've vested. Into the clouds with each round. Intellectual agreement paired with idle chatter, not enough. Action required. Time is of the essence. Earth Mother struggles for life.

Choked with pollution. Scattered with debris. Chemicals filling waterways from overindulgent and careless routines. Plagued with corporate cities and high-rise graffiti. Gentle treading and compassion, now a thing of the past. Long ago forgotten the beating in her chest. Heads selfishly turned. Immense suffering. Were we not birthed from the bosom of her girth?

We are Earth Mother. She is the beat in the cycle of life. Gifted from God. Connected to all living things as they are connected to her. Caress her. Care for her. Consider alternatives before you buy. Reduce debris. Reduce her suffering. Tend to her with love and affection.

Action required. One person independently united can make a difference. Time is of the essence.

JOYFUL EXISTENCE

Pleasures Traveled

Assumptions are made of what makes you happy. Savory pleasures tasted or gagged. Relentless attempts to manage and monopolize your time. Crafting ego-boosting social events. Those moments better spent by living *your* life.

Listen to your inner voice that beckons for reason. The inner voice that reckons with vision. Vision of a joyful existence walking *your* path and not that of another. You are one of a kind. Taste the savory existence of a life unique and exciting. You'll know when you've reached it. For you'll be *doing* instead of watching and listening.

SPRING FLOWER

Perfection

You are a beautiful spring flower amidst the thorns. Flourish you did through neglect. Unnurtured. Unadorned. Untended with the basics of love and tenderness. Struggled to thrive.

Yet there you grow. Straight. Perfect in every direction. Perfection of God's love. Delicately embellished in rosy hues. God's Light cascading from a sunset sky. Reflection of innocence. Goodness to the core.

A perfect example of opted forgiveness and spiritual growth. Casting aside blame and unanswered questions of why. Some answers forever unknown. Unwavering you remain in faith. Unlimited greatness in God's glory. Reaching for the Light. Stretching the limits.

Beautiful spring flower. Gratitude I give for my path having crossed with yours.

ABSENCE OF JUDGMENT

God's Love

Rise from the floor of torment. Extend your arms outward. Balance. Feel the warmth of God's love. Stand tall in the absence of judgment. Stand tall in the absence of assumptions. Stand tall in your decisions and direction. Stand tall in compassion and forgiveness. Stand tall.

Each person has a place. Yours different from mine. Blended energies for the greater good of all. Spread with deliberate acts of kindness and compassion. Prayerful wishes for all.

Extend your arms. Reach beyond your space. Encompass this planet. Blend your energies with mine.

Balance. Follow your heart. Echo God's love. Stand tall.

WEIGHT OF ANOTHER

Humility and Compassion

You no longer behave as the person I once knew. If honesty is still accepted, then honest I'll be. Where are you? What's happened? Quick to bite. Puffed-chest. Stroking acquisitions in a phony arena. Commanding performance. Attention-getting. Tears of compassion and forgiveness rarely gifted.

How sturdy your shoulders must be. Day after day toting a swollen personality.

Misdirected intentions.

It's not too late. If strength is what you crave, then humbly carry the weight of another. Humility and compassion are powerful actions. Allow Him into your heart. Lighten the load of yourself. Then attend to the many.

TAKE YOUR SORROW TO GOD

Comfort through Prayer

I am sorry for your loss.
You carry the sorrow and tears to fill the depths of a million oceans.

Reach to hold your hand and help I cannot. Lamenting a lifetime's of what if. . . .

Help I cannot.

Take your sorrow to God. Seek comfort with Him.

DRIFTING TO MONOTONY
Moments Unknown

I've watched for a while. Headway made across turbulent waters. Calm in sight. Then pulling in the oars. Drifting to monotony. What is it that pulls you to shore?

Fear? Fear of what? The unknown? Is not each new step taken, one-step forward you've not taken before? Fear of success? Why do you doubt the talents you've been gifted? You do not service God's highest intention by lowering your potential.

Fear not the power you hold. Fear not the path you are on. Fear not challenges or successes. You are worthy of so much more. Man your boat. Paddle from shore.

Great are your gifts. Believe in yourself and in the powers you hold.

You have purpose. Forward on. Sail to new and open waters. Joyfully live in each new moment unknown.

COMPASSION OVER REACTION

Rocky Path Taken

Assumptions made. Under the cloak of invisibility your rampage reigns. Hidden behind comments aimed to maim. Spreading rumors. Covering your trail. To what end, my friend? To what end?

Travel the path the other has taken. Until then, assumptions put to rest. The only assumption left standing is that they did their best.

We all come from a place of experiences past and present. Combination unique to each person. Take your reaction to a situation and replace it with compassion. For until opportunity presents itself that you are all knowing—you know nothing of the place from which they have come.

Replace reaction with compassion. Judge not. Harm not. For you know not the rough and rocky path they've traveled.

RENEWED FAITH

Glorious Butterfly

It is with heartfelt words of which I speak. Clarity comes during the most trying of times. Emerging from the cocoon with tear-glittered stained wings. Ready to soar. New in form. New in strength. New in attitude with an abundance of peace. Renewed in faith.

Balance yourself in God's love. Reflect on this earth journey and lessons learned.

This storm will pass. Hold tightly to God's promise. For you walk not alone.

Soar high glorious butterfly.

FACING TRAGEDY

Stronger than You Think

So gallantly you have rallied. Abrupt collision with life-altering derailment. Clinging to normalcy whilst pummeled to your knees. Searching what's left. Pieces jaggedly assembled. Reflecting the puzzle remaining. Progression of life.

Through grief and setbacks, life goes on. Facing tragedy with grace and God at your side. Your strength commended. Your inner beauty mirrored in the life you tend.

Remember when faced with solitary sadness. Promise you have been gifted. Life continues on. From this into the next.

EMOTIONAL FIELDS

Peace and Tranquility

Agitated you are of late. Uncomfortable in commonplace situations. Activities once enjoyed, now criticized. Heavily treading through plowed troughs of empty emotional fields. You tighten the wrap so carefully knotted. Shielding and stockpiling emotional collateral. Ignoring the mounting internal discontent. What is the source of your distraction?

Could it be the Universe nudging your back? Urging upward momentum in a different direction? The more you ignore—the stronger the nudges.

Matters not what brought you to this place. Matters now the path you take. Initiation from you will birth the change. Seek awareness of Him. Discontent will soon dissipate. The heaviness of life lifted through angelic embrace.

May you be graced with peace and tranquility within and about.

BORROWER OF WORDS

Blessings Shalom Aho Amen

Awake you were before the plummet from youth. To Earth-walk sleep you quickly fell. Difficult it was. Alone and heart-broken. Unaware of God's prodding. Angelic shadows passing from the corner of your eye.

You have always been wanted. You have always been loved. Your talents are urgently needed. Grandest of efforts required for the service at hand.

Blessings. Shalom. Aho. Amen.

Writer for children you are, but not the children imagined. Grown are they in stature. Mature in stance. Burden and gift it is. Not for the glamour. But the journey. The journey of others. Souls asleep at life's helm. Steering through foggy-clouded visions. Like you before the prodding began. Born they were also, awake and aware of God's love. Innocent, creative, and imaginative in the purest of form. In the purest of love.

Borrower of words. Share your gifted phrases. Nudge at the heart of sleeping souls. Their talents are urgently needed. Grandest of efforts required for the service at hand.

Blessings. Shalom. Aho. Amen.

NEW BEGINNINGS

Release to God

Stagnate you've become with thoughts and memories strewn about your feet. Thorny overgrowth covering a once tended path. Piles grow larger. Slowing the pace. Reeking of stench. Breeding ground in the shadowed shallows of the ego-laden water.

If the company you wish to keep is with justifications—ramifications—look-at-me pity written on your sleeve—then so be it! Tire yourself whilst standing knee-deep. Another option might be to wade through the muck of days past and travel higher—lighter—brighter. The choice is yours.

Step out from the knee-buckling negativity that holds you back. Step onto a new path of sunrises and sunsets.

The choice is yours.

SHADOW CAST

Eternity

You wrestle actions against the purity within. Fists clench to your brow; your heart wrenches against the thunderous pound. Dream weaves held captive by raging internal wars.

Let me ask of you this.

What shadow do you wish to cast upon the Earth? A shadow drawn to the negative pulls? A shadow of sorrow and precious moments left undone? A shadow of what could have been? A shadow of nothing more?

What shadow do you wish to cast?

Good deeds spread in a continuum for eternity. Let your shadow grow through kind words and heartfelt songs. Carry another until they are able to walk on their own.

When all is said and done, the question should be *how far has your shadow gone?*

FAITHFUL SERVICE

Constant Diligence

Troubled I am for your latent disregard. Unkind observations. Sarcastic humor. Jokes at your own expense. What is the source of your aggravation?

You are you.

Your exterior is only but a small part of what makes you special. You are beautiful and unlike another. Ever changing like the morning sky. I am saddened by your unkind attitude towards a Godly creation.

Your habits are as follows: Self-hatred, abuse, and embarrassment.

Try gratitude for a body gifting diligence of maintenance. Years of twenty-four-hour service whilst you work, sleep, and play. Gratitude for a beating heart and limbs that move. Gratitude for a voice that can sing. Gratitude for the arms to hold a troubled friend. Gratitude for a voice to spread His Light. Gratitude for your uniqueness. Gratitude for being the ever so faithful friend. Gratitude for the partnership with your soul until life's journey ends.

Take better care of your body so it can take better care of you. Love yourself, including your exterior shell.

GOD'S CREATION

Exceptionally Different

Heartsick I am for the sake of the many. Conformity. Rigidity. Living within a box. Unable to let go for fear of attention. Rejection.

What if you were to simply be you? Uniquely different in whatever form that should be. Writing poetry. Singing off-key. Dancing in the streets. Mixing plaids with prints. Puddle jumping at the age of eighty-three.

God created this planet. Every rock and blade of grass. Similar yet exceptionally different. Like sunrises and sunsets.

The uniqueness of individuals should be deemed a delight.

Let go. Be creative. Be happy and silly. Be young at heart.

For the heart of a child is close to God.

LOST CONNECTIONS

Gifted Conversation

I long for the connections of our past. Happy times engaged in laughter and silliness.

Now we mirror that which was meant to facilitate.

We worry of missed connections through beeps, rings, and typed responses.

Let me see and feel the caverns of your soul.

Meet me. Speak to me. Allow me the privilege of seeing the furrows of your brow flex and accentuate excitement or sorrow.

Leave behind the texting and messaging. I do not care for that which you ate last night or which outfit you recently bought.

I care for that which is who you are.

Are you well? Are you happy? What lessons of life have you mastered since we last spoke?

Words spoken, a commodity in rarity these days.

Were you not gifted with a tone that rings harmoniously with my soul?

Meet with me. Speak with me. Gift me conversation and the joy of your presence.

INHALING LIFE'S BLESSING

Unswaggering Intention

Impressed I am with your unswaggering intention. Striving for safe passage over upheavals personal in nature. Sight not lost on earthly direction. Focus remaining through weather-stained glasses.

Courage it takes. Inhaling all of life blessings. Holding in one's hand a precious moment of time. Guarantees not made for the length of stay. Guarantees not needed. For life continues through kind actions and intentions. Good deeds touch many. Good intentions seed the same in others. A positive attitude is contagious.

Blessings, my friend, for the journey ahead. You are my hero. My reminder of the strength carried within. Forward momentum regardless the twists and turns of the path traveled.

To all who bear witness to a similar battle, learn from my friend. Learn to give gratitude for each breath taken. Learn to remain focused through personal battles. Learn to participate in life and make positive changes for the planet. Gift of yourself for the greater good of the whole.

We walk not alone through this life and into the next. Leave behind a reflection bright enough to be seen through weather-stained glasses.

WALL OF SILENCE

Conversation Gifted

Dialogue is an important part of any relationship. Conversation is a gift when spoken with compassion and clarity. Leaving nothing unsaid. Assumptions put to rest. Agreements may be pending. But filling the heart-place with understanding and grace.

Instead, you were slapped back with attitude followed by a testy comeback. A bold and arrogant wall of silence now shrouds the remains.

Conversations gifted, that is your stance. A recommendation to everyone before things get out of hand. Agreements are not necessary. But gifted is the understanding of intentions.

So easy for some to sit on their throne of assumptions. Hiding in silence. For conversation might provide clarity of a situation. Instead, they greedily feed on misconstrued words or actions. Harboring anger. Adding layers to the thickness of silence.

You did your best. Best wishes to the other half. Go now in your own direction.

A MOTHER'S LOVE

Watercolor Celebrations

Time travels onward, distancing the present from the past. Memories sketched across crinkled paper. Pages worn and torn from travel. Sections missing. Forever vibrant and pure are the memories of my children.

To them, I send a canvas of watercolor celebrations. Carefully painted. Framed in golden lacing. Priceless. Sacred. A first breath. First haircut. First tooth. First smile. First step. Firsts of all and any reason to celebrate their coming into themselves. My life's humble journey as their parent.

For each and every day of their life, gratitude I give for witnessing the growth and expanse of their mind and talents. Growth and expanse of their individuality. Growth and expanse of their being. The *I am* moment when realizing their purpose on the planet.

At the end of my journey, may my paintings reflect a mother's love for her children. Priceless. Sacred. From their first breath to my last.

BURDENS PLACED

Dignity of You

Visible on your sleeve is the heart of a child. Efforts constant to measure up. Comparisons unjust. Preset expectations from those closely placed. Bar so high, living with hidden disgrace. Measure not to the standards of what others think or do. Stand tall in the blessing of you.

Child of God, mistakes will be made. Part of the natural process called *life*. God has put no limits on the directions you take. Heights traveled, or paths changed.

Child of God, release the kite string of *not-good-enough* tethered to your hands. Faulty expectations and comparisons are on *them*. God has gifted you talents and a path unique. Different and beautiful as each sunset. Honor Him by acknowledging this blessing.

Beauty epitomized through the uniqueness totally and remarkably *you*.

Blaming

Somber clouds hang heavy over Earth Mother. Walls erecting. Propagandized sharing. Niceties declining. Tolerance waning. Tweets reigning. Blaming for the economy. Blaming for society's decline. Blaming, blaming, blaming.

Are you not my neighbor?

Regardless of religion, location, or color of skin—are you not my neighbor? Neighbors across nations. Neighbors across oceans. Related through the Father.

Time to stop blaming. Time to stop propagandized sharing. Time to take down the walls of fear and assumptions. We are the same. Mother to mother. Father to father.

Stop the spiraling. Reach beyond the computer. Make the human connection. Extend yourself. Offer good tidings and kind actions without reason. Open a door. Smile at a stranger earnestly without worry for their preference of ballot. Wave a good morning. Wave and say, *God bless you.*

Look beyond the darkening clouds to possibilities. Neighbor

to neighbor, next door and across oceans. Light the way for another. Good will is contagious amongst neighbors.

May God's blessing follow you, my neighbor, through this day and into the next.

LONELINESS

Fullness of Heart

Loneliness plays a cruel and impartial game. It thrives on the emptiness of heart. A heart that yearns for love. Matters not how surrounded you are. Matters only that alone you feel. Wringing of hands. Pacing through life. Prisoner within yourself. Heart locked away. Lonely you will be if that is what you seek.

Companionship comes in different forms. Inconsequential greetings. A simple hello. A hug from a neighbor. Look for the fullness of life. The fullness of heart is what you will receive.

SUNRISE PROMISE

Good on the Horizon

My friend, your life and actions are unsettled as of late. An emotional volcano eager to erupt. Provocation unwarranted. Slap happy with words that ring bitter.

Come—let me give you a hug. For I see beyond the spewing anger. I see a soul in pain. I see a soul resisting the joys of God's promises just ahead on the horizon's sunrise.

My friend, you wrap yourself in a rough exterior. Using words that splinter to keep others at bay. Shielding yourself from the possibility of pain.

Come—let me give you a hug. For I see the unrest stamped upon your face. Dogged with thoughts of what should have been for your life. Let down from directions untold. Secretly holding hurts. Unmentionable of sorts.

My friend, you carry the shell of hard knocks upon a weighted back. Life's journey made difficult. No one cares—or so you think.

Come—let me give you a hug. For I see the gentle soul crying for release. The scars you bear are not yours to keep. Release to God painful memories that block your Light. Release the fears that blind you of the sunrise promise of a new day.

Guarantee I cannot that life will not stamp another injustice. But guarantee I can that there is more good than bad on life's horizon. Beautiful butterfly, spread your wings. Come from the thick cocoon of hurtful behavior. Let the world see the beauty of you and not the horrific burdens carried.

Come—let me give you a hug. I see beyond the words that ring bitter. I see a compassionate soul crying to be held. I see someone wishing to share the horizon of purple-hued colors and afraid to be alone.

My friend, welcome to life. Welcome to the arms and heart of another.

GOD'S GIFT

Life's Drum

Frustration creeps. Wryly stalking. Whilst fear wakes your restless sleep. Cycling self-doubt. All efforts wasted. The moment's gone.

My friend, the moments passed are gone, but there is always *now*. Build on this moment, then add on the next. Overwhelming rampaging emotions replaced with action and rest.

You are here for a reason. Learn your craft. It will all fall into place. Release wasted emotions. Replace them with peace. Peace in your heart. Peace in your life.

Hard work will pay off when following the right drum.

Build on this moment. Build on the now. Moment to moment. For each snippet of time is God's gift of love.

Humbly Embrace Life

Directly to your heart I reply. Ticking of minutes. Hours lost in the day. Suffering alone needlessly. Disappointments and pain. Important to remember. There is Light just beyond the storm.

Sit within the arms of God. Gently rock. Tenderly grieve. Loss. Frustration. Sadness. Then, when ready—change your pattern. Soften the heartfelt blows. Outward projection to help others will heal the soul. Help varies in degrees. Sometimes a smile is all that is needed. In moments of great despair, a smile offered restores spiritual balance. Remembrances elegantly mantled. Once painfully visual. Now adored.

Disappointment in life's follies will remain. But sadness will be replaced. In your darkest moments draw from God's Light. Peace and love. Humbly embrace life—the ups and the downs.

CONTRIBUTION TO HUMANITY

Simple Acts of Kindness

How short the life of a rose. Fragrantly alluring. Budded beauty surrounded by thorns. Long lasting is the dandelion. Self-sustaining as it changes form. Humble beauty—both the dandelion and the rose.

Gifts of the heart evolve like the bud of a rose. The generous actions of one touch the souls of the whole. Like the seeds of a dandelion blown in a storm.

Contribute to the whole. Seed to the wind kindness, generosity, hope, and encouragement. Gift of your time and talents. Pray for the afflicted and unfed. Worry not the planted location of intentions. God will tend to that.

Humble beauty is compassion.

How short the life of man. Time negotiated for acquisitions of glass houses and social status. Emotionally alluring. Budded beauty surrounded by metal thorns. Long lasting is the contribution employed. Self-sustaining as it changes form. Do for the sake of humanity. Do for the sake of your soul. Matters not whether you are a dandelion or a rose. Seeded actions of compassion blossom and bloom beyond your vision, and beyond the thorns.

BEACON OF GOD'S LIGHT

Linking of Hearts

Stand tall in the significance of you. Fuel of compassion. Boundless in innocence. Contagious with laughter. Child of God. Stand tall. Allow your Light to shine.

Let go of doubt erroneously placed. For within your heart resides the love of God. You are here for a reason. Your talents are greatly needed.

Witness. Believe. Believe in yourself as a child of God. Believe in the power of one. Believe in the linking of hearts through faith. Faith in the ability to make a difference.

Beacon of God's Light. Shine.

Shine through your actions and intentions. Walk the walk. Talk the talk. Twenty-four-seven. Child of God. You are here for a reason.

Shine.

CALMING WATERS

Life's Challenges

I've missed you. Time taken to clear your head. Time well spent, my friend. Peaceful surroundings have a calming effect. Head stops racing. Worries screech to a halt. Things of little importance can wait. Things of little importance disproportionately weighted. What's important is the trend.

What have you learned of your connection to this place? Interactions with brethren and Earth Mother? What is your interpretation of events?

Self-imposed reflection has a balancing effect. Harmonizing life's challenges. Spreading your wings in a spiritual sense.

A path vertical in nature requires a peaceful stance. Fill your heart with the calming waters of God's love.

Take the time needed. I'll be here when you get back.

EMOTIONAL CLEANSING

Release to God

There are as many reasons for tears as there are types of laughter. Tears need not be a definable symptom. Downing prescriptions or self-medication. Masking a tearful existence.

Learn to use soulful reflection. Learn to use tears to cleanse the emotional remembrance. Allow for the flow. Limit in time as to what you *know* is needed. No more. No less. Privately sorrowful in reflection.

Then wrap the sorrows in laced fabric. Tie a bow of braided gold sashes. Release to God the burden too great to carry.

Always there will be tear-filled situations. Welcome the cleansing.

ABUNDANCE GIFTED

Search with Your Heart

When was the last time you sat outdoors? Filling your lungs with God's fresh air. Regardless of what lies beneath your feet. Soil. Dust. Grass. Cement. Stone.

Look up. Look out. See the abundance God has gifted. There for the taking. Grant yourself one moment to look. Search with your heart. Feel the heavenly compassion of God everywhere.

Challenge yourself each waking day. Find the glory that awaits. Then give gratitude for each amazing day.

It is a beautiful world in which we live. To your knees you will drop when searching with your heart.

PEACEFUL EXISTENCE

Amazingly Beautiful

You balance atop an incline of emotions. Sliding into rage one moment. Clinging to sadness the next. The sensitivities you feed fester and snowball. Gathering momentum. Blocking the Light. You're out of adjustment. Thoughts and considerations beyond rationality. Stop where you are. Open your eyes.

Seek firm footing. Hold out your hands. Feel the warmth and love of God's Light. Embrace higher intentions by letting go of the ego's snowballed existence. Stop feeding the festering of ugliness that blocks your Light. Child of God. It is so much easier to be you. Anger and rage devour your strength. Leaving behind a body frail and ill. Let it go. Give it to God.

Under the blanket of emotions rests the child of God. Happy. At peace. Ready to play. Let your tears flow for the love in your heart. Cry at heartfelt exchanges instead of rage. Slide into a peaceful existence instead of fighting within your head.

It is so much easier to be you. Child of God. Amazingly gracious. Amazingly beautiful. Come, let me introduce you to yourself.

LOVE OF THE FATHER

Surrender to Serenity

Wedged in your heart is an arrow of defeat. Surrendered to circumstances delinquent. Dragging what's left of child-like laughter to the bin of rubbished debris.

My friend, surrender not to the past that weighs heavily on your heart. Surrender to peace. Surrender to God's love. Surrender to serenity.

Only you can take the first step. Willing you must be. Surrender the baggage wrapped tightly around a heart desperately trying to beat. Toss the baggage to the rubbish bin. Pull back from the rubble the child carried within.

Regardless your age or circumstance, a child you still carry. A child full of God's graces. Cry first if you must. A cleansing cry, then move on. Laugh. Rejoice. Be an example of how to live. Breathe in God's love.

Child of God, you are here for a reason.

LIFE GIFTED

Through the Looking Glass

Matters not the combo platter of letters attached. OCD or ABC. Time dedicated to the doings of others is time wasted. Time spent well, is time of your own.

What brings the greatest pleasure? Reading? Writing? Singing? Company of others?

No guarantees on the length of this journey. Waste not one moment consumed with the letters. Live your life. Step through the looking glass into your place on this planet.

There's much to explore. Paths to intersect. Actions to take of the highest order.

Live the life God has gifted. Live your life by doing and not watching others.

STUTTERING OF PEN

Gift of God

Shared problem it is. The wordsmith rollercoaster ride. One extreme to the other. Incomplete thoughts whilst you sit and stare. Stuttering of pen. Then the pen starts to ramble. Scaring the strongest of heart. Thoughts and images fill the page. Falling from the edges. *What's happening?* you wonder. Breaking the magic of the writing moment. The pen gets stuck on a verb irregular. My friend, the words will flow if you let go.

Follow through with the furrows of paper. Weaving hither and fro. Quilting tales carefully stitched. Let the story unfold. Your heart knows the direction to go.

Words written are a gift from God. Creation of a most beautiful kind. Music of a different nature. Wrapping adventures and heartfelt images around minds. Traveling the distance. Stories with intention. Messages with direction.

When the pen starts to ramble, follow the ride.

Past Traveled

My dear and special friend, I am blessed with our relationship. Synchronicity on many levels. Silence over coffee—yet volumes spoken. Tears shared for many occasions. Laughter, especially under duress. Honesty, our closest companion. We *are* friends.

As of late, your sadness shadows my heart. For what reason is the heaviness of your sorrow? Tell me not with words, for I believe I know the answer. I caught a glimpse of you in the chair, rocking. It is into the past you have traveled.

My dear friend, I am blessed with you—my special friend. Leave me not alone in this moment of time. Leave the sorrow of yesterday where it belongs. Stop rocking. Your heart and compassion are greatly missed. I ask with the greatest of affection, release the past and your sorrows to God.

I am blessed to call you friend.

GOD'S LOVE

Beauty and Innocence

Black lace drapes your face. Hidden behind. You weep. Things said or love withheld. Your heart breaks. Unworthy you feel of love and success.

My dear one, loved you have always been. Search with your heart. Feel God's embrace. You are a child of His.

Circumstances or past events dictate not the path. Weep no longer. Lift the lace. Step into you. Worthy you are. Worthy you have always been.

Courage it takes for the change. Positive in thoughts. Strong in action. Throw away the shroud. Expose the beauty and innocence. Run and play at life. This life was meant to be joyful.

Find the child within. Find the child of His. Peace and love will follow as well as success.

TOIL HAPPILY

Seriousness with Moderation

I've been in your place. Wringing of hands. Wrangling work and life. A stopwatch existence. Accepting stress with the ring of success. My friend, slow down, take a breath.

Important it is to allow for lazy days of play and misspelled words. Gallivanting in flip-flops, and dirt to your knees. Important it is to strive for work at play.

God has gifted you the spirit of a child. A desire to puddle jump and play at life. Relinquish the ruler-slapping dogma and tight-fitting regimes. There is time and space for play. For when life's obligations are viewed with grace, the work will get done at a peaceful pace.

Honor this life gifted. Toil happily. Joyfully play at work and work at play.

MIND STILL STRONG

Rainbow of Innocence

Glad I was to see you today. Selfish I am. Clinging to your cloak. Aware how tired and out of sorts you've become. Mind still strong as your body gives out. Praying for passage gently gifted from this life to the next.

Job well done, my friend. Follower of the heart. Handing off to the next in place. Rest gently, dear one, in God's warm embrace.

Remember you I will through quiet moments of reflection. Happy times. Laughter and silly notions. Childlike in your heart. The strength of a million in resolve. A rainbow of innocence stapled across a clouded sky.

Life will go on. Not the same. It is I who shall remain. Left behind alone and out of sorts.

Shine for me at Heaven's gate.

HOW TO JUDGE SUCCESS

Eliminate Comparisons

It's been a while. Absence creates a distance of time and emotional space.

Your struggle is not with the journey, but with the delivery of success. The ego grows larger than life. Comparisons made. Self-imposed judgment follows.

Eliminate comparisons.

Look to a field of wildflowers bowing gracefully in each breath of wind. Now look closely. The flowers are not the same. Some have fewer petals. Others have wilted through time. Glorious in their individual beauty. Glorious together.

Be glorious in your individual talents and beauty. Success in life is the ability to bow gracefully with each breath.

SHOW GOD TO A CHILD

Faith

A child was born. Perfection of God's love. Minus the shield and sword society places. Minus intolerance. Minus assumptions of the distinction between color and race. Minus social ladders and political gains. A child was born. Perfection of God's love.

Swaddle the young. Teach through actions instead of insults. Guide through actions instead of withholding of love.

Swaddle the young. Innocent and pure. Shine God's Light through your actions instead of abandonment of love. Show—don't tell.

Swaddle the young—be it yours or someone else's. Teach and guide through actions and intentions. Reflect God's Light. Shine God's Light. Guide the young by living a joyful life minus the sword and shield. Embrace life with peace and harmony. Allow the young to learn through their eyes and heart the perfection of God's love.

SUFFERINGS OF THE HEART

Wishes and Prayers

Wishes and prayers cannot change the past. Too many words spoken. Too much time lapsed. Typhoon choices destroying delicate balance. Overshadowing sweet bouquets of tender moments shared.

Wishes and prayers cannot change the past. Honest reflection laced with forgiveness can. Acknowledge your part. Open your heart to forgiveness.

Sufferings of the heart are long lasted. Like the typhoon, gathering collateral. Forgive your loved one. Forgive yourself. Learn from mistakes. Learn to take not one moment for granted.

Send a sweet bouquet of rose-scented bubbles. Each bubble representing a tender moment shared. For each bubble popped, that moment remembered. Ask from your heart for forgiveness and imagine it granted. Then pick up the phone and speak from a place of honesty and heartfelt emotion.

Wishes and prayers cannot change the past. Prayers and reflection can.

Perpetuate Peace

I see your challenges. Direction to decide. Future in hand. It is not my place. Urging one way or another. Bearings you will find when following the heart-place.

Carried within are the answers you seek. Listen in the quiet moments. Believe in yourself and the trail straight and bright.

There are no rights or wrongs. Where to live. The job to take. Simply variations of the trails of life. To what benefit to the human race is the question you might ask. Any path, when followed with grace, will serve the greater good of the whole and the greater good of you.

Satisfaction you will find, my friend, when in a place of peace.

FOLLOW GOD'S LIGHT

Calm Waters

Life's been a long haul. Tossed about. Near drownings of your own accord. Choosing to sail rough waters over wading through the calm. The storms grow darker. It is the Universe with a wake-up call.

Take the first step. Leave your muddy shoes freckled on shore. Float through life on good deeds, different choices, and God's love.

You are here for a reason. Cling no longer to a broken hull. Storms will come—but quickly pass. Learn to follow God's Light to calmer waters.

Blessings to you on this gifted day.

REIGNING SOVEREIGN

Look beyond Yourself

Must be nice. Must be nice to live in your world. Reigning sovereign. So perfect. Never having made a mistake. How nice it must be to hand down the verdict. Withholder of love. Tenderness misplaced. Judging from within the limited experience of a narrow existence. Withholder of love, your behavior borders torturous.

How nice it would be if you would listen with your greatest gift. Compassion. Heartfelt compassion towards the actions and decisions of others. Instead of judging their life's ripple against the shores of your life.

Look, dear one, beyond yourself. See the wake of *your* actions. Not quite so easy to penalize when clearly looking at oneself. The world is full of intersecting paths. You know not their crooked trail traveled or the intentions of their actions.

Regain balance through positive intentions. Positive actions. Become a giver of love and compassion. Use the greatest gift God intended. Compassion towards yourself and others.

DISTRACTION

Enjoy the Moment

Distraction. What a dirty word. Delaying you from the par-laying of your work. Distraction. Pulling hither and fro. Distraction. Frustration mounts. Angry words spew. Distraction—or reminder there's more to life.

Birds chirp regardless of deadlines. Babies cry wanting for attention. The wind blows sweet breezes just enough to rattle papers. These are the reminders there's more to life. More than paychecks and deadlines. More than climbing social ladders. More than bank accounts and falling stock prices. There's so much more.

Priceless is the music of nature. Priceless is the neck cuddle with a baby. Priceless are God's reminders to stop—stop—stop and enjoy the moment.

Allow for a pull hither and fro. For one moment spent in gratitude for a gentle distraction is the balance and energizer for a giant step forward.

GOD IS NOT A POLITICIAN

Gentle and Sweet

I offer compassion for the place in which you sit. Wedged against a wall of vices. Knowing and believing from different directions. My friend, the angst you feel is separation from God's love.

Stop the bantering thoughts. Release your sadness. There is a place for you upon this planet. Feel His love. Hear His voice. Not loud or boisterous. God is not a politician—but a gentle and sweet reminder of love and compassion.

Follow His Light. Fill your heart and life with His presence. Shine brightly in your actions.

Shine brightly, my friend. Every beacon is needed.

NEWS REPORTS AND POLLS

Lost in Translation

I see a gentle reminder is in order. If political persuasion is the purpose of your pounding conversation—this is all I hear regarding news reports and polls. *Blah, blah, blah—and blah.* Important may be your message, but the gist gets lost in *my* translation.

Tell me instead of reports pertaining to children with remarkable talents, goodness, earth-shattering and significant achievements. Tell me of crooning voices like angels. Musicians orchestrating whilst connected in heart to Heaven. Report to me of good Samaritans feeding the homeless. Heroes rescuing children. Saints caring for the aged. Report to me the remarkable feats of teachers, preachers, writers, and speakers. Tell me of a tweet or post that is uplifting, enlightening, humorous, heart touching or soul moving.

To all these things I will gladly tune in. Everything else gets lost in my translation.

Knowing and Believing

Words will never express the gravity of emotion. For with my eyes, I no longer tend the vision of your smile. With my arms, I no longer feel your embrace.

So, my dear one, with my heart I extend. Finding you in moments abated. You are the wind and morning dew. The morning's sunrise and sunset's kiss good night. You are the laughter of children. Birds in flight.

The promise given from God. This time known as life continues in motion. So patiently, I await. Focusing on positives. Knowing and believing. You and I again shall again embrace.

OVERCOME AGING

Learn to Love Life

I know the calling. Time has a way of playing cruel tricks on the body. Sagging parts that never before existed. Furrows etched through experience. Skin that hangs in outrageous places. Headset in the twenties whilst the knees and back scream, *take the elevator!* How many times bent and twisted mopping floors and lifting children?

I know the calling. My friend, time does have a way of playing cruel tricks on the body.

But with the degradation of the body comes a richness of the soul. Lessons and sorrows. Blessed memories. Headset in the twenties aligned with a heart strong and full. Understandings of serenity. Focus outward and upward for life's calling.

Time has a way of playing cruel tricks on the body. But, my friend, did you ever see so well before? Beyond the near and far-sightedness of your youth to the priceless vision of God's sunrises and sunsets. To see through hallowed vision the rainbow of life. To see the needy as God's children. To see and understand the rise and fall of life's lessons. To see when to offer patience. To see the richness of our planet and the possibilities that time has to offer.

Tell me, dear friend, did you ever see so well before?

POWER OF PRAYER

Lighting a Path

Let me pray with you. Let the tears run free. Let me embrace you across the sea. We are here together. Friends a world apart. Supporting. Guiding. Lifting. Lighting the way through the dark.

Join with me in prayerful union. For together we can do anything. Limit not our intentions selfishly. Include in dialogue those suffering. Peace to their hearts. Peace to their souls. May circumstances provide miracles, so they know they are not alone.

Let me pray with you. Let the tears run free. Together join hands across the sea. Brothers and sisters united unselfishly in God's Light. Supporting. Guiding. Lifting.

Lighting a path for all to see.

Let me pray with you.

MEDIA'S DISTORTIONS

Be Bold

You stand behind a fan unfolded. Mirrored reflection distorted. Never measuring up. Unfair. Unjust. A shadowed existence. Hidden within yourself.

Be bold. Drop appearances. Stand on your own.

The distortion you see is of your own making. Levy not against what you think you should be. Simply *be*. Overflowing you are in all of God's graces. Beauty, intelligence, and talents galore. Unique to yourself.

Be bold. Drop appearances. Stand on your own.

Reflect not your friends or television celebrities. Reflect the Light God has so blessed in thee. Your talents are greatly needed.

Be bold. Drop appearances. Stand on your own. Child of God, see what God sees in thee.

PRECIOUS MOMENTS LOST

Hope for Today

I've sat in your seat. Sound asleep. Unaware of the abundance presented before closed eyes. Precious moments lost. Forgiveness requested. For searching the past is a waste of time. Sorrow for what is lost. Hope for today. Grateful I am to finally awaken.

So grateful am I. Abundance from the Universe pours from every direction. Every inch of Earth Mother a serious wonder. Not to mention humankind. Potentials grand when compassionately driven.

Take in three deep breaths. Close your eyes. Sit for a moment. A moment you surely have. Search with your heart. To tears you will be driven. For within your heart-place you will find an abundance of love and compassion. Now look about. See what God sees. Harmony and compassion our greatest potential. When finally we awaken.

EMPTY PROMISES

False Voices

Politicians. False voices echoing across expanses. Promises void intention. Politicians, the less attention given, the better. Waste not on the rich-of-self. For within their golden fortress resides emptiness.

Take charge of *your* energy. Let not the state-of-the-nation address your spiritual place. Campaign for the starving and homeless. Campaign for families that go without. Campaign for a unity of souls. Allow your voice to be heard through your prayerful songs. Sing for humanity. Sing for all nations. Sing prayers for the planet.

You hold the power of God's Light. Shine through the deluge of negatives that surround the planet. Your Light will shine brighter when combined with mine. Together we can make a difference.

Shine brighter. Pray with intensity and compassion. Live in harmony with your brethren and the planet. There will always be self-crowned kings in places of power. The less attention given, the better.

LOST SECOND CHANCE

Faith

Drapes drawn. Cloaked in black. Mourning a lost second chance.

Sometimes in this life . . . there are no second chances. Circumstances change. People pass-over. Hearts harden. Lost opportunities sway as *if only* like golden wheat in the wind.

So, there you are. Drapes drawn. Cloaked in black. Mourning a lost second chance.

This is the time when faith steps in. Faith that heartache will pass. Faith that God's love will follow you all the days of your life and into the next.

My friend, mourn no longer for lost second chances. Rejoice for lessons learned and the avoidance of the need for second chances.

TEARS CONCEALED

Journey of Grief

Wipe the tears so carefully concealed as before when out and about. Returning home, alone you sit. Solitude slammed on the doorstep of peace. My friend, alone you will never be. For God tends your needs whilst you grieve.

Personal and private is the journey of grief. Family's worrisome chatter offers little relief. Sit with God. Give to God the burden carried. Overwhelming emptiness to the edges of your space. Pray for release. Release from heartache and sorrow. Release from grief.

Allow in God's Light. Promise you have. Life continues on. Here and thereafter.

Search your heart place. Feel God's embrace.

OPEN YOUR HEART

Walk in God's Light

Sadly you sit. Perched behind lace. Your heart locked behind the gate of a synthetic cage. Shackled ankles dragging the past. Watching from afar the life journey of neighbors.

You hold the key to set yourself free. Think hard. Search with your heart. Remember the reason God gifted life. Transition from pain. Transition from sadness. Think hard, dear one. You are here for a reason.

Let go of the past. Let go of the if-only and what-if. That was then. This is now. Pull back from the curtains. Learn to live *your* life. Open the door to this moment in time. Fear not the future. The future will unfold in a most peaceful way if only you will unlock your heart and let go of the past.

Join the life journey with neighbors. Take my hand. We will walk together. I'll shield the darkness as you walk in Light.

There are no guarantees for the length of your stay. Leave behind man-made injuries and pain. Leave behind insecurities and choices poorly made. Walk in God's Light. Set yourself free.

ABANDONMENT

God's Love

It comes in many forms. It drops men to their knees. It leaves children crying. It alters the self-esteem. It brings the heart to an unhappy place.

Abandonment is a form of abusive. Abandonment of love. Abandonment of conversation. Abandonment of heartfelt connections.

There are times when distance *is* the best course of action. But abandonment used as punishment is torture. Torture that leaves hearts broken. Lights flicker. Souls wander. Fears take over.

My friend, you walk not alone. God's love and attention have never faltered. Forgive. Move on. Give your heart to God. Rise from your knees. Wipe your tears. You have always been loved.

You are never alone.

PREACHER SPEAKER WRITER TEACHER

Gentle Soul

The sun breaks through as the rain dances. Butterflies kiss an extended hand. Words blossom forth from mere intention. A peaceful existence in all life actions. A gentle soul—the preacher, speaker, writer, teacher.

Angels rejoiced at the birth. This world a better place. For a gentle soul now tends Earth Mother. Tending through words gifted and carefully placed.

The sun breaks through as the rain dances. God's gifted travel through the sharing and bending of words and phrases. Blended emotions carried on the wings of butterflies to the blossomed flowers of the imagination.

A gentle soul— the preacher, speaker, writer, teacher. Graced with God's blessings. Joyfully playing in God's garden of a blossoming imagination.

LIFE LESSONS LEARNED

Stumbles

If I had only known. Different instructions I would have given to my children when they were young. To them I would have said that each step taken is a lesson learned. Stumbles are normal. Some tumbles larger than others. Falls are expected. Perfection is not required. You are here for a reason.

If only I had known. Different expectations I would have had for myself. I would have known to get up after a fall. Perfection was not required. I was put here for a reason.

If only we knew. We would have done different. But we didn't. We were learning through falls and stumbles. Regardless the tumbles taken, find comfort in the knowledge that perfection is not expected. Learn from life's stumbles. Be an example. Carry compassion in your heart for yourself and all the steps taken. Falls are expected.

You are here for a reason. Learn life lessons.

FORGIVENESS GIFTED

Seeds of a Dandelion

Opportunities escape through the passage of time. Heartfelt messages left unsaid. Cold your heart remains. Dripping of tears not expressed. Anger unyielding. Forgiveness disintegrates.

To what purpose does it serve?

Your point made. Sentencing passed. Punishment delivered. Silence—silence—silence.

The clock still ticking.

There are no guarantees for the distance we travel. Journeys end in a flash. Ravaging the cold-hearted. Leaving a barrel loaded with *if only* and *now* it's too late.

Another option there is. Forgiveness from the heart warm and yielding. From a place of higher intentions. From compassion.

Forgiveness gifted.

Forgiveness spread like the seeds of a dandelion.

FOCUS ON GOD'S LIGHT

Shadowed Images

Troubling it is—the overhead view of this place in which we live. Violence. Disruption. Paranoia. Fear spreading across waters. Look closer—but with blinded eyes. See with your heart. See beyond the shadowed images. See and feel the peaceful rumblings of humble hearts uniting.

Shine from your place of sovereignty, your Light combining with mine. Actions of the highest order. Peaceful proclamations. Assumptions and negative intentions swept to the side. Overpowering the shadows with God's bright Light.

Change of focus is the first step. For it is that in which you seek you shall find. Look for God's Light spreading across waters. Look for the good in people and circumstances. Give gratitude for this moment of time.

Troubling it is—the overhead view of this place in which we live. Mind the shadowed images but focus on God's Light. The world needs your gentleness of heart. The world needs your Light.

ANGST BLANKETS OUR NATION

Prayer and Intention

Angst blankets our nation. Brothers and sisters tightly wound in the propaganda of politics. A strong nation requires unity of hearts and prayers.

Release the escalating tensions with prayer. Pray for Divine intervention when required. Pray for what truly matters. Children fed. Homeless with shelter. Shadows of darkness replaced with peaceful nations.

And, if agitation persists, back up your prayers with intentions. Take action. Tend to the elderly sequestered from society. Read to a child. Gift of yourself. You have so much to offer.

Angst and politics—they go hand in hand. Prayer and intention—another direction.

DREAM SING DANCE WRITE DRAW

Mind Heart and Soul

Weathered are the hands that toil day after day. Heavy is the heart that worries through the night. Stagnant is the creativity that fears to be caught less than perfect.

The work can wait. Push worries to the side. Gift to yourself freely and without guilt the time needed to create. What is it that makes time stand still? Dreams, songs, dance, words, art?

Create the intention of play. Follow it by action. Create as you did when you were a kid. Think back. Have you ever seen a child push away time to paint? Time to sing? Time to dream? Time to dance? Time to use the imagination that God has gifted? Have you ever seen a child afraid to play? Afraid of being caught playing less than perfect?

Play is play. There are no standards of measurement of play. Play is the freedom to create with the mind, heart, and soul. There are no wrongs or rights. Work will seem easier. Worries turn to Light. The heart beats stronger.

Time allotted for creativity opens the gateway for happiness. Lift your heart. Simply create!

DREAM

Path of Prayer

I know the depth of your pain. Hurt. Misled. Changing the course of a path earlier taken. Then abruptly—dead-ended. Manipulated by a charlatan of many colors. It didn't turn out as expected.

Leave behind unfulfilled dreams and wishes. Leave behind the unkind words and actions. Leave behind all the *what-ifs* and *should-have-beens*. Change direction.

Put forward your intentions of the highest order. Mind not those of the other. Karma's dues will boomerang back. Regain your power.

You hold within the power of the Universe. Impose *your* destiny. A path of peace, serenity, gifting, giving, loving, forgiving, and learning.

Give gratitude, for each day is a blessing. Sadness is expected. Remember, this time will pass. Lesson learned. Onto the next.

Find peace within your space. Dream big. Always dreams of your own.

PASSING OF A LOVED ONE

Forever Missed

It is a place I try to avoid. Remembering the last moments of a life so vividly worn. Laughter and love freely gifted. Taken too soon. Taken without warning.

The visual I fight of the last days clearly numbered. The pain of death written and worn. The body failed as the spirit sought freedom to soar. Childhood memories laced with peace for a journey's ending.

The fight disappeared as the body dissolved. Muffled whispers surged like waves on the beach. A soon empty house overflowing. Quiet sobbing layered with patronizing well wishes. A squeeze of the hand. Too tired to fight. Too tired to sing.

Then peace gifted.

POLLYANNA PINK SUNSET

After the Fight

Bleak is the emotional charge left after a fight. Captured moments of tenderness either forgotten or thrown to the wind. Heart bleeding. Why fight?

Resolution might be better served with a velvet voice linked to receptive ears.

Allow Pollyanna pink sunsets to put to rest the discourse from your day. Step back from the ego-driven conversation and listen. To what value does fighting add to your life or to that of another? Look to other options. Compromise and forgiveness.

There are no guarantees for your length of stay on this planet. Miss not one glorious Pollyanna pink sunset or Pollyanna pink option in life. Put your ego to sleep. Hold tight to your faith. The rest will fall into place.

DISRUPTION

Spotlight Brilliance

The absence of clarity. It brings down nations. It causes dis-
harmony in a once harmonized house. It distances children
from parents, sisters from brothers. Absence of clarity. It creates
foggy dead-end trails. It causes disruption in life paths and wedges
hearts against God.

If only situations could be seen from another perspective.
The personality clashes would no longer exist. Life paths would
be adorned with spotlight brilliance.

The absence of clarity exists if you allow it.

Step out of yourself. See with your heart the reasons and whys
of a situation. Open your heart and end the disruption in your
life. Clarity always follows.

JOYFUL REUNION

A Lifetime of Love

My heart skips a beat. Your happiness is apparent. Reunion of hearts once entwined many lifetimes ago. Your souls finagled the joyful event.

Follow youthful dreams. Silver-haired makes no matter. Run through life's fields unencumbered. Joyfully laughing. Having fun. Hearts beating as one. Lifting the spirits of those still sleeping. Giving thanks for God's blessings.

Hold hands through the journey of life's bumps and ruts. Stay close and forever happy this lifetime and into the next.

Many lifetimes exist within one.

WAKE-UP CALL

Live Life

Hurriedly, you toss moment to moment into what's coming. The checklist mounts on your drafted life table. Meanwhile, pink zebra-striped mornings escape your vision.

Slow down. Stop thinking. Start living.

Checklists are important in order for goals to manifest into reality. Energy and effort are required for things to get done. But, what of the moment that just passed *unnoticed?*

Balance dreams with an effort at living. Take time to notice pink zebra striped mornings and butterfly flower kisses. Work happily and efficiently towards your checklist, but leave time to notice God's blessings.

Live life. See life. Be life. Do life. Work hard while living fully. Don't let the moment escape your vision.

Path to God

Tenderly gifted you are with verse. Lighting the path to God's love and hope. Helping wayward souls find their way home. Home to God.

Blessings to you for efforts exerted. Alone with thought. Alone with words. But alone you are not, for the passing of messages links you to the lives touched. Lifting, carrying, prodding, encouraging. Need for recognition need not be given. For within your gift is the tightly wound connection to God.

Unifier of hearts. Unifier of religions. Unifier of peoples. Speakers, teachers, writers, and preachers. Blessings to you for efforts exerted.

Acknowledgements

I am forever grateful for my connection with God. May His gifted words be a blessing and a gentle nudge to those seeking His presence.

Thank you to my son, Timothy J. Cassano, for suggesting I write a blog—for through those early entries my spiritual voice was found.

Thank you to Timothy C. Smith for never-ending love and encouragement.

Thank you to final readers Kathy Scorse, Lily Tanzer, Cairn McCormack, and Mary B. Love for offering words of encouragement, insights, and reviews.

To friends Sam Attardo and Nancy Atherton, thank you for the tender encouragement that saw me through three years of twisting and turning words into verse.

I would like to thank my publicist, Denise Cassino, for seeing the simplicity of thought and serenity of heart in my work. Thank you for urging me to publish *Spiritual Verse Today*.

Thank you to Chris O'Byrne and the formatting team from *JETLAUNCH* Book Design for a wonderful experience and fantastic finished product. Special thanks to Debbie O'Byrne for another amazing cover design.

Thank you to Andrea Page and Darcy Pattison for opening the door to blogging and website management.

Thank you to special friend Nancy Pistorius for your encouragement across time and distance.

I am grateful for all your efforts sending me off and on my way on another life journey. You are a gift and deeply cherished.

With warm regards,
—Sharon CassanoLochman

Index

A Mother's Love *Watercolor Celebrations*, 107
Abandonment *God's Love*, 148
Absence of Judgment *God's Love*, 89
Abundance Gifted *Search with Your Heart*, 121
Accept the Journey *Words for the Writer*, 45
Alone at Your Desk *Journeyman Days near the End*, 4
Angst Blankets Our Nation *Prayer and Intention*, 153
Beacon of God's Light *Linking of Hearts*, 118
Beautiful Soul *Friend*, 47
Believe *Good Deeds*, 55
Blaming and Excuses *Forgiveness Love Compassion*, 63
Blanket of Light *Depths of Depression*, 41
Borrower of Words *Blessings Shalom Aho Amen*, 97
Burdens Placed *Dignity of You*, 108
Calming Waters *Life's Challenges*, 119
Challenges Faced *God's Light*, 73
Challenges Unannounced *Walk in God's Light*, 68
Child of God *Let Go of the Past*, 31
Clouded Mirror *Brilliant Beauty*, 21

Compassion over Reaction *Rocky Path Taken*, 93
Contribution to Humanity *Simple Acts of Kindness*, 116
Darkness *Unite in Light*, 46
Disruption *Spotlight Brilliance*, 159
Distinctions Unique *Perfection Inside and Out*, 81
Distractions *Enjoy the Moment*, 136
Door of Possibilities *Amazing Life Awaits*, 66
Drama and Chaos *Spiritual Well*, 6
Dream *Path of Prayer*, 156
Dream Sing Dance Write Draw *Mind Heart and Soul*, 154
Drifting to Monotony *Moments Unknown*, 92
Drudgery of Life *Child's Play*, 72
Earthly Obligations *Forever be Joyful*, 10
Emotional Cleansing *Release to God*, 120
Emotional Fields *Peace and Tranquility*, 96
Emotional Ties *Strength from the Universe*, 25
Empty Belly *Sustainability*, 62
Empty Promises *False Voices*, 144
Facing Tragedy *Stronger than You Think*, 95
Faithful Service *Constant Diligence*, 101
False Smiles *Expense of Another*, 57
False Surface *Hidden Shame*, 50
Fear of Heartache *Allow God's Light*, 53
Focus on God's Light *Shadowed Images*, 152
Follow God's Light *Calm Waters*, 134
Forgiveness Gifted *Seeds of a Dandelion*, 151
Free as a Spring Butterfly *Released*, 77
Free-Spirited Butterfly *Keeper of Light*, 7
Future in Hand *Perpetuate Peace*, 133
Gifted of God *All Living Things*, 86
God is not a Politician *Gentle and Sweet*, 137
God's Creation *Exceptionally Different*, 102
God's Gift *Life's Drum*, 114
God's Love *Beauty and Innocence*, 127
Gratitude for God's Blessings *Beauty of the Moment*, 17
Gratitude this Holiday Season *Prayerful Wishes*, 33

Gratitude to God *Embrace Differences*, 1
Gratitude *Union with God*, 85
Grief Suffering Sadness *Humbly Embrace Life*, 115
Harsh Tone *Trumpets across Nations*, 59
Haze of Life *Life's Journey*, 20
Heavenly Goal *Seek God*, 44
Heavenly Warrior *Peace Needed*, 5
How to Judge Success *Eliminate Comparisons*, 130
Human Connection *Blaming*, 109
Ignorance of Youth *Forever of Tomorrows*, 37
Industrialized Sleep *Balance for Humanity*, 23
Inhaling Life's Blessing *Unswaggering Intention*, 104
Journal with the Mind *Blessings of Nature*, 30
Joyful Existence *Pleasures Traveled*, 87
Joyful Reunion *A Lifetime of Love*, 160
Knowledge *Honor God*, 48
Let God Carry Your Burdens *Seek Personal Peace*, 43
Life Gifted *Through the Looking Glass*, 124
Life Lessons Learned *Stumbles*, 150
Loneliness *Fullness of Heart*, 111
Lost Connections *Gifted Conversation*, 103
Lost Second Chance *Faith*, 145
Love Freely Given *God by Your Side*, 61
Love of the Father *Surrender to Serenity*, 123
Media's Distortions *Be Bold*, 142
Memories Cycled *Forgiveness*, 80
Messages of Hope *Words Unhindered*, 28
Mind Still Strong *Rainbow of Innocence*, 129
Minding the Gate *Love Yourself and Neighbors*, 29
Mission Statement *Live Life by Example*, 14
Moments of Uncertainty *Harmonious Intentions*, 34
New Beginnings *Let in the Light*, 27
New Beginnings *Release to God*, 99
News Reports and Polls *Lost in Translation*, 138
Nourish Your Soul *Strive for Spiritual Health*, 64
Once Majestic Nation *Way of Life*, 78

One Less Tick Upon the Clock *Passing of a Loved One,* 8
Open Your Heart *Walk in God's Light,* 147
Overcome Aging *Learn to Love Life,* 140
Passing of a Loved One *Forever Missed,* 157
Peaceful Existence *Amazingly Beautiful,* 122
Perfection to Your Core *Breath of God Gave Life,* 18
Pink Leopard Sunrise *Give Gratitude,* 83
Playful Living *Company of Others,* 13
Pollyanna Pink Sunset *After the Fight,* 158
Power of Prayer *Lighting a Path,* 141
Pray for Miracles *Pink Pinafores and Overalls,* 39
Praying for Answers *Magnitude of Cries,* 9
Preacher Speaker Writer Teacher *Gentle Soul,* 149
Precious Moments Lost *Hope for Today,* 143
Promise Given *Knowing and Believing,* 139
Refuge in God's Blessings *Cowardly Chatter,* 26
Reigning Sovereign *Look beyond Yourself,* 135
Renewed Faith *Glorious Butterfly,* 94
Restless Sleep *Awake,* 74
Sacrifices Made *Sorrowful Cries,* 75
Sadness of Heart *Past Traveled,* 126
Scuffles with Thought *Compassion and Forgiveness,* 70
Search with Your Heart *Compassion,* 54
Shadow Cast *Eternity,* 100
Shattered Health *New Realizations,* 22
Show God to a Child *Faith,* 131
Sit Watch Click *Child's Play,* 38
Slippery Depth *Ego's Sanctions,* 67
Sorrow to Shed *Heartbeat of Humanity,* 69
Sorrowful and Listless *The Perplexities of Life,* 51
Speakers Teachers Writers Preachers *Path to God,* 162
Spring Flower *Perfection,* 88
Stammering and Sputtering *Issue Repeats,* 76
Stress *Butterfly Light,* 36
Stuttering of Pen *Gift of God,* 125
Sufferings of the Heart *Wishes and Prayers,* 132

Sunrise Promise *Good on the Horizon*, 112
Surge of Words *Release Fear*, 65
Surrender to Your Sorrow *Shadowed Darkness*, 11
Take Your Sorrow to God *Comfort through Prayer*, 91
Tears Concealed *Journey of Grief*, 146
Tender Messages *Write Speak Sing Praise*, 56
Time of Need *Midst of Fire*, 52
Times of Struggle *Pray for Strength*, 35
Toil Happily *Seriousness with Moderation*, 128
Topsy-Turvy *Hold Firm with Grace*, 60
Trembling of Faith *Pray*, 84
Uniting in Faith *Children of God*, 15
Wake-Up Call *Live Life*, 161
Walk with God *Life's Storms*, 3
Wall of Silence *Conversation Gifted*, 106
We are One *Speaker Teacher Preacher Writer*, 16
Wedged on the Threshold *Amazing Life Awaits*, 49
Wedged to the Past *Pray*, 58
Weight of Another *Humility and Compassion*, 90
Words Straining to Flee *Cadence Needed*, 2

About the Author

Sharon CassanoLochman is a spinner of drama, tailor of emotions, manipulator of personal connections, and a player of words. She writes for the spiritually minded and the young at heart. She is the author of **Spiritual Verse Today**, **Man with the Sand Dollar Face**, and **Stranded on Thin Ice**. To learn more about Sharon CassanoLochman visit her website at sharoncassanolochman.com.

24422009R00104

Made in the USA
Columbia, SC
23 August 2018